CHALLENG

Records of re

CW00506872

DATE	TIME	PERSON REFUSED	PRODUCT/COMMENTS	AGED FOR ID	REFUSED BY/SIGNED
....../....../......	:	MALE.................. ☐ FEMALE.............. ☐	REASON: COMMENTS:	YES: ☐ NO: ☐	STAFF NAME: SIGNED:

DATE	TIME	PERSON REFUSED	PRODUCT/COMMENTS	AGED FOR ID	REFUSED BY/SIGNED
....../....../......	:	MALE.................. ☐ FEMALE.............. ☐	REASON: COMMENTS:	YES: ☐ NO: ☐	STAFF NAME: SIGNED:

DATE	TIME	PERSON REFUSED	PRODUCT/COMMENTS	AGED FOR ID	REFUSED BY/SIGNED
....../....../......	:	MALE.................. ☐ FEMALE.............. ☐	REASON: COMMENTS:	YES: ☐ NO: ☐	STAFF NAME: SIGNED:

DATE	TIME	PERSON REFUSED	PRODUCT/COMMENTS	AGED FOR ID	REFUSED BY/SIGNED
....../....../......	:	MALE.................. ☐ FEMALE.............. ☐	REASON: COMMENTS:	YES: ☐ NO: ☐	STAFF NAME: SIGNED:

DATE	TIME	PERSON REFUSED	PRODUCT/COMMENTS	AGED FOR ID	REFUSED BY/SIGNED
....../....../......	:	MALE.................. ☐ FEMALE.............. ☐	REASON: COMMENTS:	YES: ☐ NO: ☐	STAFF NAME: SIGNED:

DATE	TIME	PERSON REFUSED	PRODUCT/COMMENTS	AGED FOR ID	REFUSED BY/SIGNED
....../....../......	:	MALE.................. ☐ FEMALE.............. ☐	REASON: COMMENTS:	YES: ☐ NO: ☐	STAFF NAME: SIGNED:

CHALLENGE 25
Records of refusals

DATE	TIME	PERSON REFUSED	PRODUCT/COMMENTS	AGED FOR ID	REFUSED BY/SIGNED
....../....../......	:	MALE.................. ☐ FEMALE.............☐	REASON: COMMENTS:	YES: ☐ NO: ☐	STAFF NAME: SIGNED:

DATE	TIME	PERSON REFUSED	PRODUCT/COMMENTS	AGED FOR ID	REFUSED BY/SIGNED
....../....../......	:	MALE.................. ☐ FEMALE.............☐	REASON: COMMENTS:	YES: ☐ NO: ☐	STAFF NAME: SIGNED:

DATE	TIME	PERSON REFUSED	PRODUCT/COMMENTS	AGED FOR ID	REFUSED BY/SIGNED
....../....../......	:	MALE.................. ☐ FEMALE.............☐	REASON: COMMENTS:	YES: ☐ NO: ☐	STAFF NAME: SIGNED:

DATE	TIME	PERSON REFUSED	PRODUCT/COMMENTS	AGED FOR ID	REFUSED BY/SIGNED
....../....../......	:	MALE.................. ☐ FEMALE.............☐	REASON: COMMENTS:	YES: ☐ NO: ☐	STAFF NAME: SIGNED:

DATE	TIME	PERSON REFUSED	PRODUCT/COMMENTS	AGED FOR ID	REFUSED BY/SIGNED
....../....../......	:	MALE.................. ☐ FEMALE.............☐	REASON: COMMENTS:	YES: ☐ NO: ☐	STAFF NAME: SIGNED:

DATE	TIME	PERSON REFUSED	PRODUCT/COMMENTS	AGED FOR ID	REFUSED BY/SIGNED
....../....../......	:	MALE.................. ☐ FEMALE.............☐	REASON: COMMENTS:	YES: ☐ NO: ☐	STAFF NAME: SIGNED:

CHALLENGE 25
Records of refusals

DATE	TIME	PERSON REFUSED	PRODUCT/COMMENTS	AGED FOR ID	REFUSED BY/SIGNED
....../ ....../	:	MALE.................☐ FEMALE..............☐	REASON: COMMENTS:	YES: ☐ NO: ☐	STAFF NAME: SIGNED:

DATE	TIME	PERSON REFUSED	PRODUCT/COMMENTS	AGED FOR ID	REFUSED BY/SIGNED
....../ ....../	:	MALE.................☐ FEMALE..............☐	REASON: COMMENTS:	YES: ☐ NO: ☐	STAFF NAME: SIGNED:

DATE	TIME	PERSON REFUSED	PRODUCT/COMMENTS	AGED FOR ID	REFUSED BY/SIGNED
....../ ....../	:	MALE.................☐ FEMALE..............☐	REASON: COMMENTS:	YES: ☐ NO: ☐	STAFF NAME: SIGNED:

DATE	TIME	PERSON REFUSED	PRODUCT/COMMENTS	AGED FOR ID	REFUSED BY/SIGNED
....../ ....../	:	MALE.................☐ FEMALE..............☐	REASON: COMMENTS:	YES: ☐ NO: ☐	STAFF NAME: SIGNED:

DATE	TIME	PERSON REFUSED	PRODUCT/COMMENTS	AGED FOR ID	REFUSED BY/SIGNED
....../ ....../	:	MALE.................☐ FEMALE..............☐	REASON: COMMENTS:	YES: ☐ NO: ☐	STAFF NAME: SIGNED:

DATE	TIME	PERSON REFUSED	PRODUCT/COMMENTS	AGED FOR ID	REFUSED BY/SIGNED
....../ ....../	:	MALE.................☐ FEMALE..............☐	REASON: COMMENTS:	YES: ☐ NO: ☐	STAFF NAME: SIGNED:

CHALLENGE 25
Records of refusals

DATE	TIME	PERSON REFUSED	PRODUCT/COMMENTS	AGED FOR ID	REFUSED BY/SIGNED
....../....../......	:	MALE................☐ FEMALE..............☐	REASON: COMMENTS:	YES: ☐ NO: ☐	STAFF NAME: SIGNED:

DATE	TIME	PERSON REFUSED	PRODUCT/COMMENTS	AGED FOR ID	REFUSED BY/SIGNED
....../....../......	:	MALE................☐ FEMALE..............☐	REASON: COMMENTS:	YES: ☐ NO: ☐	STAFF NAME: SIGNED:

DATE	TIME	PERSON REFUSED	PRODUCT/COMMENTS	AGED FOR ID	REFUSED BY/SIGNED
....../....../......	:	MALE................☐ FEMALE..............☐	REASON: COMMENTS:	YES: ☐ NO: ☐	STAFF NAME: SIGNED:

DATE	TIME	PERSON REFUSED	PRODUCT/COMMENTS	AGED FOR ID	REFUSED BY/SIGNED
....../....../......	:	MALE................☐ FEMALE..............☐	REASON: COMMENTS:	YES: ☐ NO: ☐	STAFF NAME: SIGNED:

DATE	TIME	PERSON REFUSED	PRODUCT/COMMENTS	AGED FOR ID	REFUSED BY/SIGNED
....../....../......	:	MALE................☐ FEMALE..............☐	REASON: COMMENTS:	YES: ☐ NO: ☐	STAFF NAME: SIGNED:

DATE	TIME	PERSON REFUSED	PRODUCT/COMMENTS	AGED FOR ID	REFUSED BY/SIGNED
....../....../......	:	MALE................☐ FEMALE..............☐	REASON: COMMENTS:	YES: ☐ NO: ☐	STAFF NAME: SIGNED:

CHALLENGE 25
Records of refusals

🚫18

DATE	TIME	PERSON REFUSED	PRODUCT/COMMENTS	AGED FOR ID	REFUSED BY/SIGNED
....../....../......	:	MALE................. ☐ FEMALE............... ☐	REASON: COMMENTS:	YES: ☐ NO: ☐	STAFF NAME: SIGNED:

DATE	TIME	PERSON REFUSED	PRODUCT/COMMENTS	AGED FOR ID	REFUSED BY/SIGNED
....../....../......	:	MALE................. ☐ FEMALE............... ☐	REASON: COMMENTS:	YES: ☐ NO: ☐	STAFF NAME: SIGNED:

DATE	TIME	PERSON REFUSED	PRODUCT/COMMENTS	AGED FOR ID	REFUSED BY/SIGNED
....../....../......	:	MALE................. ☐ FEMALE............... ☐	REASON: COMMENTS:	YES: ☐ NO: ☐	STAFF NAME: SIGNED:

DATE	TIME	PERSON REFUSED	PRODUCT/COMMENTS	AGED FOR ID	REFUSED BY/SIGNED
....../....../......	:	MALE................. ☐ FEMALE............... ☐	REASON: COMMENTS:	YES: ☐ NO: ☐	STAFF NAME: SIGNED:

DATE	TIME	PERSON REFUSED	PRODUCT/COMMENTS	AGED FOR ID	REFUSED BY/SIGNED
....../....../......	:	MALE................. ☐ FEMALE............... ☐	REASON: COMMENTS:	YES: ☐ NO: ☐	STAFF NAME: SIGNED:

DATE	TIME	PERSON REFUSED	PRODUCT/COMMENTS	AGED FOR ID	REFUSED BY/SIGNED
....../....../......	:	MALE................. ☐ FEMALE............... ☐	REASON: COMMENTS:	YES: ☐ NO: ☐	STAFF NAME: SIGNED:

CHALLENGE 25
Records of refusals

DATE	TIME	PERSON REFUSED	PRODUCT/COMMENTS	AGED FOR ID	REFUSED BY/SIGNED
....../....../......	:	MALE.................. ☐ FEMALE.............. ☐	REASON: COMMENTS:	YES: ☐ NO: ☐	STAFF NAME: SIGNED:

DATE	TIME	PERSON REFUSED	PRODUCT/COMMENTS	AGED FOR ID	REFUSED BY/SIGNED
....../....../......	:	MALE.................. ☐ FEMALE.............. ☐	REASON: COMMENTS:	YES: ☐ NO: ☐	STAFF NAME: SIGNED:

DATE	TIME	PERSON REFUSED	PRODUCT/COMMENTS	AGED FOR ID	REFUSED BY/SIGNED
....../....../......	:	MALE.................. ☐ FEMALE.............. ☐	REASON: COMMENTS:	YES: ☐ NO: ☐	STAFF NAME: SIGNED:

DATE	TIME	PERSON REFUSED	PRODUCT/COMMENTS	AGED FOR ID	REFUSED BY/SIGNED
....../....../......	:	MALE.................. ☐ FEMALE.............. ☐	REASON: COMMENTS:	YES: ☐ NO: ☐	STAFF NAME: SIGNED:

DATE	TIME	PERSON REFUSED	PRODUCT/COMMENTS	AGED FOR ID	REFUSED BY/SIGNED
....../....../......	:	MALE.................. ☐ FEMALE.............. ☐	REASON: COMMENTS:	YES: ☐ NO: ☐	STAFF NAME: SIGNED:

DATE	TIME	PERSON REFUSED	PRODUCT/COMMENTS	AGED FOR ID	REFUSED BY/SIGNED
....../....../......	:	MALE.................. ☐ FEMALE.............. ☐	REASON: COMMENTS:	YES: ☐ NO: ☐	STAFF NAME: SIGNED:

CHALLENGE 25
Records of refusals

DATE	TIME	PERSON REFUSED	PRODUCT/COMMENTS	AGED FOR ID	REFUSED BY/SIGNED
....../....../......	:	MALE................☐ FEMALE..............☐	REASON: COMMENTS:	YES: ☐ NO: ☐	STAFF NAME: SIGNED:

DATE	TIME	PERSON REFUSED	PRODUCT/COMMENTS	AGED FOR ID	REFUSED BY/SIGNED
....../....../......	:	MALE................☐ FEMALE..............☐	REASON: COMMENTS:	YES: ☐ NO: ☐	STAFF NAME: SIGNED:

DATE	TIME	PERSON REFUSED	PRODUCT/COMMENTS	AGED FOR ID	REFUSED BY/SIGNED
....../....../......	:	MALE................☐ FEMALE..............☐	REASON: COMMENTS:	YES: ☐ NO: ☐	STAFF NAME: SIGNED:

DATE	TIME	PERSON REFUSED	PRODUCT/COMMENTS	AGED FOR ID	REFUSED BY/SIGNED
....../....../......	:	MALE................☐ FEMALE..............☐	REASON: COMMENTS:	YES: ☐ NO: ☐	STAFF NAME: SIGNED:

DATE	TIME	PERSON REFUSED	PRODUCT/COMMENTS	AGED FOR ID	REFUSED BY/SIGNED
....../....../......	:	MALE................☐ FEMALE..............☐	REASON: COMMENTS:	YES: ☐ NO: ☐	STAFF NAME: SIGNED:

DATE	TIME	PERSON REFUSED	PRODUCT/COMMENTS	AGED FOR ID	REFUSED BY/SIGNED
....../....../......	:	MALE................☐ FEMALE..............☐	REASON: COMMENTS:	YES: ☐ NO: ☐	STAFF NAME: SIGNED:

CHALLENGE 25
Records of refusals

🚫18

DATE	TIME	PERSON REFUSED	PRODUCT/COMMENTS	AGED FOR ID	REFUSED BY/SIGNED
....../....../......	:	MALE...............☐ FEMALE...........☐	REASON: COMMENTS:	YES: ☐ NO: ☐	STAFF NAME: SIGNED:

DATE	TIME	PERSON REFUSED	PRODUCT/COMMENTS	AGED FOR ID	REFUSED BY/SIGNED
....../....../......	:	MALE...............☐ FEMALE...........☐	REASON: COMMENTS:	YES: ☐ NO: ☐	STAFF NAME: SIGNED:

DATE	TIME	PERSON REFUSED	PRODUCT/COMMENTS	AGED FOR ID	REFUSED BY/SIGNED
....../....../......	:	MALE...............☐ FEMALE...........☐	REASON: COMMENTS:	YES: ☐ NO: ☐	STAFF NAME: SIGNED:

DATE	TIME	PERSON REFUSED	PRODUCT/COMMENTS	AGED FOR ID	REFUSED BY/SIGNED
....../....../......	:	MALE...............☐ FEMALE...........☐	REASON: COMMENTS:	YES: ☐ NO: ☐	STAFF NAME: SIGNED:

DATE	TIME	PERSON REFUSED	PRODUCT/COMMENTS	AGED FOR ID	REFUSED BY/SIGNED
....../....../......	:	MALE...............☐ FEMALE...........☐	REASON: COMMENTS:	YES: ☐ NO: ☐	STAFF NAME: SIGNED:

DATE	TIME	PERSON REFUSED	PRODUCT/COMMENTS	AGED FOR ID	REFUSED BY/SIGNED
....../....../......	:	MALE...............☐ FEMALE...........☐	REASON: COMMENTS:	YES: ☐ NO: ☐	STAFF NAME: SIGNED:

CHALLENGE 25
Records of refusals

DATE	TIME	PERSON REFUSED	PRODUCT/COMMENTS	AGED FOR ID	REFUSED BY/SIGNED
....../....../......	:	MALE................□ FEMALE.............□	REASON: COMMENTS:	YES: □ NO: □	STAFF NAME: SIGNED:

DATE	TIME	PERSON REFUSED	PRODUCT/COMMENTS	AGED FOR ID	REFUSED BY/SIGNED
....../....../......	:	MALE................□ FEMALE.............□	REASON: COMMENTS:	YES: □ NO: □	STAFF NAME: SIGNED:

DATE	TIME	PERSON REFUSED	PRODUCT/COMMENTS	AGED FOR ID	REFUSED BY/SIGNED
....../....../......	:	MALE................□ FEMALE.............□	REASON: COMMENTS:	YES: □ NO: □	STAFF NAME: SIGNED:

DATE	TIME	PERSON REFUSED	PRODUCT/COMMENTS	AGED FOR ID	REFUSED BY/SIGNED
....../....../......	:	MALE................□ FEMALE.............□	REASON: COMMENTS:	YES: □ NO: □	STAFF NAME: SIGNED:

DATE	TIME	PERSON REFUSED	PRODUCT/COMMENTS	AGED FOR ID	REFUSED BY/SIGNED
....../....../......	:	MALE................□ FEMALE.............□	REASON: COMMENTS:	YES: □ NO: □	STAFF NAME: SIGNED:

DATE	TIME	PERSON REFUSED	PRODUCT/COMMENTS	AGED FOR ID	REFUSED BY/SIGNED
....../....../......	:	MALE................□ FEMALE.............□	REASON: COMMENTS:	YES: □ NO: □	STAFF NAME: SIGNED:

CHALLENGE 25
Records of refusals

DATE	TIME	PERSON REFUSED	PRODUCT/COMMENTS	AGED FOR ID	REFUSED BY/SIGNED
....../....../......	:	MALE.................. ☐ FEMALE.............☐	REASON: COMMENTS:	YES: ☐ NO: ☐	STAFF NAME: SIGNED:

DATE	TIME	PERSON REFUSED	PRODUCT/COMMENTS	AGED FOR ID	REFUSED BY/SIGNED
....../....../......	:	MALE.................. ☐ FEMALE.............☐	REASON: COMMENTS:	YES: ☐ NO: ☐	STAFF NAME: SIGNED:

DATE	TIME	PERSON REFUSED	PRODUCT/COMMENTS	AGED FOR ID	REFUSED BY/SIGNED
....../....../......	:	MALE.................. ☐ FEMALE.............☐	REASON: COMMENTS:	YES: ☐ NO: ☐	STAFF NAME: SIGNED:

DATE	TIME	PERSON REFUSED	PRODUCT/COMMENTS	AGED FOR ID	REFUSED BY/SIGNED
....../....../......	:	MALE.................. ☐ FEMALE.............☐	REASON: COMMENTS:	YES: ☐ NO: ☐	STAFF NAME: SIGNED:

DATE	TIME	PERSON REFUSED	PRODUCT/COMMENTS	AGED FOR ID	REFUSED BY/SIGNED
....../....../......	:	MALE.................. ☐ FEMALE.............☐	REASON: COMMENTS:	YES: ☐ NO: ☐	STAFF NAME: SIGNED:

DATE	TIME	PERSON REFUSED	PRODUCT/COMMENTS	AGED FOR ID	REFUSED BY/SIGNED
....../....../......	:	MALE.................. ☐ FEMALE.............☐	REASON: COMMENTS:	YES: ☐ NO: ☐	STAFF NAME: SIGNED:

CHALLENGE 25
Records of refusals

DATE	TIME	PERSON REFUSED	PRODUCT/COMMENTS	AGED FOR ID	REFUSED BY/SIGNED
....../ ....../	:	MALE................ ☐ FEMALE.............☐	REASON: COMMENTS:	YES: ☐ NO: ☐	STAFF NAME: SIGNED:

DATE	TIME	PERSON REFUSED	PRODUCT/COMMENTS	AGED FOR ID	REFUSED BY/SIGNED
....../ ....../	:	MALE................ ☐ FEMALE.............☐	REASON: COMMENTS:	YES: ☐ NO: ☐	STAFF NAME: SIGNED:

DATE	TIME	PERSON REFUSED	PRODUCT/COMMENTS	AGED FOR ID	REFUSED BY/SIGNED
....../ ....../	:	MALE................ ☐ FEMALE.............☐	REASON: COMMENTS:	YES: ☐ NO: ☐	STAFF NAME: SIGNED:

DATE	TIME	PERSON REFUSED	PRODUCT/COMMENTS	AGED FOR ID	REFUSED BY/SIGNED
....../ ....../	:	MALE................ ☐ FEMALE.............☐	REASON: COMMENTS:	YES: ☐ NO: ☐	STAFF NAME: SIGNED:

DATE	TIME	PERSON REFUSED	PRODUCT/COMMENTS	AGED FOR ID	REFUSED BY/SIGNED
....../ ....../	:	MALE................ ☐ FEMALE.............☐	REASON: COMMENTS:	YES: ☐ NO: ☐	STAFF NAME: SIGNED:

DATE	TIME	PERSON REFUSED	PRODUCT/COMMENTS	AGED FOR ID	REFUSED BY/SIGNED
....../ ....../	:	MALE................ ☐ FEMALE.............☐	REASON: COMMENTS:	YES: ☐ NO: ☐	STAFF NAME: SIGNED:

CHALLENGE 25
Records of refusals

DATE	TIME	PERSON REFUSED	PRODUCT/COMMENTS	AGED FOR ID	REFUSED BY/SIGNED
....../....../......	:	MALE.................. ☐ FEMALE.............. ☐	REASON: COMMENTS:	YES: ☐ NO: ☐	STAFF NAME: SIGNED:

DATE	TIME	PERSON REFUSED	PRODUCT/COMMENTS	AGED FOR ID	REFUSED BY/SIGNED
....../....../......	:	MALE.................. ☐ FEMALE.............. ☐	REASON: COMMENTS:	YES: ☐ NO: ☐	STAFF NAME: SIGNED:

DATE	TIME	PERSON REFUSED	PRODUCT/COMMENTS	AGED FOR ID	REFUSED BY/SIGNED
....../....../......	:	MALE.................. ☐ FEMALE.............. ☐	REASON: COMMENTS:	YES: ☐ NO: ☐	STAFF NAME: SIGNED:

DATE	TIME	PERSON REFUSED	PRODUCT/COMMENTS	AGED FOR ID	REFUSED BY/SIGNED
....../....../......	:	MALE.................. ☐ FEMALE.............. ☐	REASON: COMMENTS:	YES: ☐ NO: ☐	STAFF NAME: SIGNED:

DATE	TIME	PERSON REFUSED	PRODUCT/COMMENTS	AGED FOR ID	REFUSED BY/SIGNED
....../....../......	:	MALE.................. ☐ FEMALE.............. ☐	REASON: COMMENTS:	YES: ☐ NO: ☐	STAFF NAME: SIGNED:

DATE	TIME	PERSON REFUSED	PRODUCT/COMMENTS	AGED FOR ID	REFUSED BY/SIGNED
....../....../......	:	MALE.................. ☐ FEMALE.............. ☐	REASON: COMMENTS:	YES: ☐ NO: ☐	STAFF NAME: SIGNED:

CHALLENGE 25
Records of refusals

DATE	TIME	PERSON REFUSED	PRODUCT/COMMENTS	AGED FOR ID	REFUSED BY/SIGNED
...../ ....../	:	MALE................. ☐ FEMALE............. ☐	REASON: COMMENTS:	YES: ☐ NO: ☐	STAFF NAME: SIGNED:

DATE	TIME	PERSON REFUSED	PRODUCT/COMMENTS	AGED FOR ID	REFUSED BY/SIGNED
...../ ....../	:	MALE................. ☐ FEMALE............. ☐	REASON: COMMENTS:	YES: ☐ NO: ☐	STAFF NAME: SIGNED:

DATE	TIME	PERSON REFUSED	PRODUCT/COMMENTS	AGED FOR ID	REFUSED BY/SIGNED
...../ ....../	:	MALE................. ☐ FEMALE............. ☐	REASON: COMMENTS:	YES: ☐ NO: ☐	STAFF NAME: SIGNED:

DATE	TIME	PERSON REFUSED	PRODUCT/COMMENTS	AGED FOR ID	REFUSED BY/SIGNED
...../ ....../	:	MALE................. ☐ FEMALE............. ☐	REASON: COMMENTS:	YES: ☐ NO: ☐	STAFF NAME: SIGNED:

DATE	TIME	PERSON REFUSED	PRODUCT/COMMENTS	AGED FOR ID	REFUSED BY/SIGNED
...../ ....../	:	MALE................. ☐ FEMALE............. ☐	REASON: COMMENTS:	YES: ☐ NO: ☐	STAFF NAME: SIGNED:

DATE	TIME	PERSON REFUSED	PRODUCT/COMMENTS	AGED FOR ID	REFUSED BY/SIGNED
...../ ....../	:	MALE................. ☐ FEMALE............. ☐	REASON: COMMENTS:	YES: ☐ NO: ☐	STAFF NAME: SIGNED:

CHALLENGE 25
Records of refusals

DATE	TIME	PERSON REFUSED	PRODUCT/COMMENTS	AGED FOR ID	REFUSED BY/SIGNED
....../....../......	:	MALE................. ☐ FEMALE.............. ☐	REASON: COMMENTS:	YES: ☐ NO: ☐	STAFF NAME: SIGNED:

DATE	TIME	PERSON REFUSED	PRODUCT/COMMENTS	AGED FOR ID	REFUSED BY/SIGNED
....../....../......	:	MALE................. ☐ FEMALE.............. ☐	REASON: COMMENTS:	YES: ☐ NO: ☐	STAFF NAME: SIGNED:

DATE	TIME	PERSON REFUSED	PRODUCT/COMMENTS	AGED FOR ID	REFUSED BY/SIGNED
....../....../......	:	MALE................. ☐ FEMALE.............. ☐	REASON: COMMENTS:	YES: ☐ NO: ☐	STAFF NAME: SIGNED:

DATE	TIME	PERSON REFUSED	PRODUCT/COMMENTS	AGED FOR ID	REFUSED BY/SIGNED
....../....../......	:	MALE................. ☐ FEMALE.............. ☐	REASON: COMMENTS:	YES: ☐ NO: ☐	STAFF NAME: SIGNED:

DATE	TIME	PERSON REFUSED	PRODUCT/COMMENTS	AGED FOR ID	REFUSED BY/SIGNED
....../....../......	:	MALE................. ☐ FEMALE.............. ☐	REASON: COMMENTS:	YES: ☐ NO: ☐	STAFF NAME: SIGNED:

DATE	TIME	PERSON REFUSED	PRODUCT/COMMENTS	AGED FOR ID	REFUSED BY/SIGNED
....../....../......	:	MALE................. ☐ FEMALE.............. ☐	REASON: COMMENTS:	YES: ☐ NO: ☐	STAFF NAME: SIGNED:

CHALLENGE 25
Records of refusals

DATE	TIME	PERSON REFUSED	PRODUCT/COMMENTS	AGED FOR ID	REFUSED BY/SIGNED
....../....../......	:	MALE.................. ☐ FEMALE.............☐	REASON: COMMENTS:	YES: ☐ NO: ☐	STAFF NAME: SIGNED:

DATE	TIME	PERSON REFUSED	PRODUCT/COMMENTS	AGED FOR ID	REFUSED BY/SIGNED
....../....../......	:	MALE.................. ☐ FEMALE.............☐	REASON: COMMENTS:	YES: ☐ NO: ☐	STAFF NAME: SIGNED:

DATE	TIME	PERSON REFUSED	PRODUCT/COMMENTS	AGED FOR ID	REFUSED BY/SIGNED
....../....../......	:	MALE.................. ☐ FEMALE.............☐	REASON: COMMENTS:	YES: ☐ NO: ☐	STAFF NAME: SIGNED:

DATE	TIME	PERSON REFUSED	PRODUCT/COMMENTS	AGED FOR ID	REFUSED BY/SIGNED
....../....../......	:	MALE.................. ☐ FEMALE.............☐	REASON: COMMENTS:	YES: ☐ NO: ☐	STAFF NAME: SIGNED:

DATE	TIME	PERSON REFUSED	PRODUCT/COMMENTS	AGED FOR ID	REFUSED BY/SIGNED
....../....../......	:	MALE.................. ☐ FEMALE.............☐	REASON: COMMENTS:	YES: ☐ NO: ☐	STAFF NAME: SIGNED:

DATE	TIME	PERSON REFUSED	PRODUCT/COMMENTS	AGED FOR ID	REFUSED BY/SIGNED
....../....../......	:	MALE.................. ☐ FEMALE.............☐	REASON: COMMENTS:	YES: ☐ NO: ☐	STAFF NAME: SIGNED:

CHALLENGE 25
Records of refusals

DATE	TIME	PERSON REFUSED	PRODUCT/COMMENTS	AGED FOR ID	REFUSED BY/SIGNED
....../....../......	:	MALE...............☐ FEMALE...............☐	REASON: COMMENTS:	YES: ☐ NO: ☐	STAFF NAME: SIGNED:

DATE	TIME	PERSON REFUSED	PRODUCT/COMMENTS	AGED FOR ID	REFUSED BY/SIGNED
....../....../......	:	MALE...............☐ FEMALE...............☐	REASON: COMMENTS:	YES: ☐ NO: ☐	STAFF NAME: SIGNED:

DATE	TIME	PERSON REFUSED	PRODUCT/COMMENTS	AGED FOR ID	REFUSED BY/SIGNED
....../....../......	:	MALE...............☐ FEMALE...............☐	REASON: COMMENTS:	YES: ☐ NO: ☐	STAFF NAME: SIGNED:

DATE	TIME	PERSON REFUSED	PRODUCT/COMMENTS	AGED FOR ID	REFUSED BY/SIGNED
....../....../......	:	MALE...............☐ FEMALE...............☐	REASON: COMMENTS:	YES: ☐ NO: ☐	STAFF NAME: SIGNED:

DATE	TIME	PERSON REFUSED	PRODUCT/COMMENTS	AGED FOR ID	REFUSED BY/SIGNED
....../....../......	:	MALE...............☐ FEMALE...............☐	REASON: COMMENTS:	YES: ☐ NO: ☐	STAFF NAME: SIGNED:

DATE	TIME	PERSON REFUSED	PRODUCT/COMMENTS	AGED FOR ID	REFUSED BY/SIGNED
....../....../......	:	MALE...............☐ FEMALE...............☐	REASON: COMMENTS:	YES: ☐ NO: ☐	STAFF NAME: SIGNED:

CHALLENGE 25
Records of refusals

DATE	TIME	PERSON REFUSED	PRODUCT/COMMENTS	AGED FOR ID	REFUSED BY/SIGNED
....../ ....../	:	MALE.................☐ FEMALE.............☐	REASON: COMMENTS:	YES: ☐ NO: ☐	STAFF NAME: SIGNED:

DATE	TIME	PERSON REFUSED	PRODUCT/COMMENTS	AGED FOR ID	REFUSED BY/SIGNED
....../ ....../	:	MALE.................☐ FEMALE.............☐	REASON: COMMENTS:	YES: ☐ NO: ☐	STAFF NAME: SIGNED:

DATE	TIME	PERSON REFUSED	PRODUCT/COMMENTS	AGED FOR ID	REFUSED BY/SIGNED
....../ ....../	:	MALE.................☐ FEMALE.............☐	REASON: COMMENTS:	YES: ☐ NO: ☐	STAFF NAME: SIGNED:

DATE	TIME	PERSON REFUSED	PRODUCT/COMMENTS	AGED FOR ID	REFUSED BY/SIGNED
....../ ....../	:	MALE.................☐ FEMALE.............☐	REASON: COMMENTS:	YES: ☐ NO: ☐	STAFF NAME: SIGNED:

DATE	TIME	PERSON REFUSED	PRODUCT/COMMENTS	AGED FOR ID	REFUSED BY/SIGNED
....../ ....../	:	MALE.................☐ FEMALE.............☐	REASON: COMMENTS:	YES: ☐ NO: ☐	STAFF NAME: SIGNED:

DATE	TIME	PERSON REFUSED	PRODUCT/COMMENTS	AGED FOR ID	REFUSED BY/SIGNED
....../ ....../	:	MALE.................☐ FEMALE.............☐	REASON: COMMENTS:	YES: ☐ NO: ☐	STAFF NAME: SIGNED:

CHALLENGE 25
Records of refusals

18

DATE	TIME	PERSON REFUSED	PRODUCT/COMMENTS	AGED FOR ID	REFUSED BY/SIGNED
....../....../......	:	MALE.................. ☐ FEMALE.............☐	REASON: COMMENTS:	YES: ☐ NO: ☐	STAFF NAME: SIGNED:

DATE	TIME	PERSON REFUSED	PRODUCT/COMMENTS	AGED FOR ID	REFUSED BY/SIGNED
....../....../......	:	MALE.................. ☐ FEMALE.............☐	REASON: COMMENTS:	YES: ☐ NO: ☐	STAFF NAME: SIGNED:

DATE	TIME	PERSON REFUSED	PRODUCT/COMMENTS	AGED FOR ID	REFUSED BY/SIGNED
....../....../......	:	MALE.................. ☐ FEMALE.............☐	REASON: COMMENTS:	YES: ☐ NO: ☐	STAFF NAME: SIGNED:

DATE	TIME	PERSON REFUSED	PRODUCT/COMMENTS	AGED FOR ID	REFUSED BY/SIGNED
....../....../......	:	MALE.................. ☐ FEMALE.............☐	REASON: COMMENTS:	YES: ☐ NO: ☐	STAFF NAME: SIGNED:

DATE	TIME	PERSON REFUSED	PRODUCT/COMMENTS	AGED FOR ID	REFUSED BY/SIGNED
....../....../......	:	MALE.................. ☐ FEMALE.............☐	REASON: COMMENTS:	YES: ☐ NO: ☐	STAFF NAME: SIGNED:

DATE	TIME	PERSON REFUSED	PRODUCT/COMMENTS	AGED FOR ID	REFUSED BY/SIGNED
....../....../......	:	MALE.................. ☐ FEMALE.............☐	REASON: COMMENTS:	YES: ☐ NO: ☐	STAFF NAME: SIGNED:

CHALLENGE 25
Records of refusals

DATE	TIME	PERSON REFUSED	PRODUCT/COMMENTS	AGED FOR ID	REFUSED BY/SIGNED
....../ ....../	:	MALE.................. ☐ FEMALE.............. ☐	REASON: COMMENTS:	YES: ☐ NO: ☐	STAFF NAME: SIGNED:

DATE	TIME	PERSON REFUSED	PRODUCT/COMMENTS	AGED FOR ID	REFUSED BY/SIGNED
....../ ....../	:	MALE.................. ☐ FEMALE.............. ☐	REASON: COMMENTS:	YES: ☐ NO: ☐	STAFF NAME: SIGNED:

DATE	TIME	PERSON REFUSED	PRODUCT/COMMENTS	AGED FOR ID	REFUSED BY/SIGNED
....../ ....../	:	MALE.................. ☐ FEMALE.............. ☐	REASON: COMMENTS:	YES: ☐ NO: ☐	STAFF NAME: SIGNED:

DATE	TIME	PERSON REFUSED	PRODUCT/COMMENTS	AGED FOR ID	REFUSED BY/SIGNED
....../ ....../	:	MALE.................. ☐ FEMALE.............. ☐	REASON: COMMENTS:	YES: ☐ NO: ☐	STAFF NAME: SIGNED:

DATE	TIME	PERSON REFUSED	PRODUCT/COMMENTS	AGED FOR ID	REFUSED BY/SIGNED
....../ ....../	:	MALE.................. ☐ FEMALE.............. ☐	REASON: COMMENTS:	YES: ☐ NO: ☐	STAFF NAME: SIGNED:

DATE	TIME	PERSON REFUSED	PRODUCT/COMMENTS	AGED FOR ID	REFUSED BY/SIGNED
....../ ....../	:	MALE.................. ☐ FEMALE.............. ☐	REASON: COMMENTS:	YES: ☐ NO: ☐	STAFF NAME: SIGNED:

CHALLENGE 25
Records of refusals 🚫18

DATE	TIME	PERSON REFUSED	PRODUCT/COMMENTS	AGED FOR ID	REFUSED BY/SIGNED
....../....../......	:	MALE.................☐ FEMALE.............☐	REASON: COMMENTS:	YES: ☐ NO: ☐	STAFF NAME: SIGNED:

DATE	TIME	PERSON REFUSED	PRODUCT/COMMENTS	AGED FOR ID	REFUSED BY/SIGNED
....../....../......	:	MALE.................☐ FEMALE.............☐	REASON: COMMENTS:	YES: ☐ NO: ☐	STAFF NAME: SIGNED:

DATE	TIME	PERSON REFUSED	PRODUCT/COMMENTS	AGED FOR ID	REFUSED BY/SIGNED
....../....../......	:	MALE.................☐ FEMALE.............☐	REASON: COMMENTS:	YES: ☐ NO: ☐	STAFF NAME: SIGNED:

DATE	TIME	PERSON REFUSED	PRODUCT/COMMENTS	AGED FOR ID	REFUSED BY/SIGNED
....../....../......	:	MALE.................☐ FEMALE.............☐	REASON: COMMENTS:	YES: ☐ NO: ☐	STAFF NAME: SIGNED:

DATE	TIME	PERSON REFUSED	PRODUCT/COMMENTS	AGED FOR ID	REFUSED BY/SIGNED
....../....../......	:	MALE.................☐ FEMALE.............☐	REASON: COMMENTS:	YES: ☐ NO: ☐	STAFF NAME: SIGNED:

DATE	TIME	PERSON REFUSED	PRODUCT/COMMENTS	AGED FOR ID	REFUSED BY/SIGNED
....../....../......	:	MALE.................☐ FEMALE.............☐	REASON: COMMENTS:	YES: ☐ NO: ☐	STAFF NAME: SIGNED:

CHALLENGE 25
Records of refusals

DATE	TIME	PERSON REFUSED	PRODUCT/COMMENTS	AGED FOR ID	REFUSED BY/SIGNED
....../....../......	:	MALE.................. ☐ FEMALE.............. ☐	REASON: COMMENTS:	YES: ☐ NO: ☐	STAFF NAME: SIGNED:

DATE	TIME	PERSON REFUSED	PRODUCT/COMMENTS	AGED FOR ID	REFUSED BY/SIGNED
....../....../......	:	MALE.................. ☐ FEMALE.............. ☐	REASON: COMMENTS:	YES: ☐ NO: ☐	STAFF NAME: SIGNED:

DATE	TIME	PERSON REFUSED	PRODUCT/COMMENTS	AGED FOR ID	REFUSED BY/SIGNED
....../....../......	:	MALE.................. ☐ FEMALE.............. ☐	REASON: COMMENTS:	YES: ☐ NO: ☐	STAFF NAME: SIGNED:

DATE	TIME	PERSON REFUSED	PRODUCT/COMMENTS	AGED FOR ID	REFUSED BY/SIGNED
....../....../......	:	MALE.................. ☐ FEMALE.............. ☐	REASON: COMMENTS:	YES: ☐ NO: ☐	STAFF NAME: SIGNED:

DATE	TIME	PERSON REFUSED	PRODUCT/COMMENTS	AGED FOR ID	REFUSED BY/SIGNED
....../....../......	:	MALE.................. ☐ FEMALE.............. ☐	REASON: COMMENTS:	YES: ☐ NO: ☐	STAFF NAME: SIGNED:

DATE	TIME	PERSON REFUSED	PRODUCT/COMMENTS	AGED FOR ID	REFUSED BY/SIGNED
....../....../......	:	MALE.................. ☐ FEMALE.............. ☐	REASON: COMMENTS:	YES: ☐ NO: ☐	STAFF NAME: SIGNED:

CHALLENGE 25
Records of refusals

DATE	TIME	PERSON REFUSED	PRODUCT/COMMENTS	AGED FOR ID	REFUSED BY/SIGNED
....../....../......	:	MALE.................. ☐ FEMALE.............☐	REASON: COMMENTS:	YES: ☐ NO: ☐	STAFF NAME: SIGNED:

DATE	TIME	PERSON REFUSED	PRODUCT/COMMENTS	AGED FOR ID	REFUSED BY/SIGNED
....../....../......	:	MALE.................. ☐ FEMALE.............☐	REASON: COMMENTS:	YES: ☐ NO: ☐	STAFF NAME: SIGNED:

DATE	TIME	PERSON REFUSED	PRODUCT/COMMENTS	AGED FOR ID	REFUSED BY/SIGNED
....../....../......	:	MALE.................. ☐ FEMALE.............☐	REASON: COMMENTS:	YES: ☐ NO: ☐	STAFF NAME: SIGNED:

DATE	TIME	PERSON REFUSED	PRODUCT/COMMENTS	AGED FOR ID	REFUSED BY/SIGNED
....../....../......	:	MALE.................. ☐ FEMALE.............☐	REASON: COMMENTS:	YES: ☐ NO: ☐	STAFF NAME: SIGNED:

DATE	TIME	PERSON REFUSED	PRODUCT/COMMENTS	AGED FOR ID	REFUSED BY/SIGNED
....../....../......	:	MALE.................. ☐ FEMALE.............☐	REASON: COMMENTS:	YES: ☐ NO: ☐	STAFF NAME: SIGNED:

DATE	TIME	PERSON REFUSED	PRODUCT/COMMENTS	AGED FOR ID	REFUSED BY/SIGNED
....../....../......	:	MALE.................. ☐ FEMALE.............☐	REASON: COMMENTS:	YES: ☐ NO: ☐	STAFF NAME: SIGNED:

CHALLENGE 25
Records of refusals

DATE	TIME	PERSON REFUSED	PRODUCT/COMMENTS	AGED FOR ID	REFUSED BY/SIGNED
....../....../......	:	MALE................ ☐ FEMALE............... ☐	REASON: COMMENTS:	YES: ☐ NO: ☐	STAFF NAME: SIGNED:

DATE	TIME	PERSON REFUSED	PRODUCT/COMMENTS	AGED FOR ID	REFUSED BY/SIGNED
....../....../......	:	MALE................ ☐ FEMALE............... ☐	REASON: COMMENTS:	YES: ☐ NO: ☐	STAFF NAME: SIGNED:

DATE	TIME	PERSON REFUSED	PRODUCT/COMMENTS	AGED FOR ID	REFUSED BY/SIGNED
....../....../......	:	MALE................ ☐ FEMALE............... ☐	REASON: COMMENTS:	YES: ☐ NO: ☐	STAFF NAME: SIGNED:

DATE	TIME	PERSON REFUSED	PRODUCT/COMMENTS	AGED FOR ID	REFUSED BY/SIGNED
....../....../......	:	MALE................ ☐ FEMALE............... ☐	REASON: COMMENTS:	YES: ☐ NO: ☐	STAFF NAME: SIGNED:

DATE	TIME	PERSON REFUSED	PRODUCT/COMMENTS	AGED FOR ID	REFUSED BY/SIGNED
....../....../......	:	MALE................ ☐ FEMALE............... ☐	REASON: COMMENTS:	YES: ☐ NO: ☐	STAFF NAME: SIGNED:

DATE	TIME	PERSON REFUSED	PRODUCT/COMMENTS	AGED FOR ID	REFUSED BY/SIGNED
....../....../......	:	MALE................ ☐ FEMALE............... ☐	REASON: COMMENTS:	YES: ☐ NO: ☐	STAFF NAME: SIGNED:

CHALLENGE 25
Records of refusals

DATE	TIME	PERSON REFUSED	PRODUCT/COMMENTS	AGED FOR ID	REFUSED BY/SIGNED
....../....../.......	:	MALE.................☐ FEMALE.............☐	REASON: COMMENTS:	YES: ☐ NO: ☐	STAFF NAME: SIGNED:

DATE	TIME	PERSON REFUSED	PRODUCT/COMMENTS	AGED FOR ID	REFUSED BY/SIGNED
....../....../.......	:	MALE.................☐ FEMALE.............☐	REASON: COMMENTS:	YES: ☐ NO: ☐	STAFF NAME: SIGNED:

DATE	TIME	PERSON REFUSED	PRODUCT/COMMENTS	AGED FOR ID	REFUSED BY/SIGNED
....../....../.......	:	MALE.................☐ FEMALE.............☐	REASON: COMMENTS:	YES: ☐ NO: ☐	STAFF NAME: SIGNED:

DATE	TIME	PERSON REFUSED	PRODUCT/COMMENTS	AGED FOR ID	REFUSED BY/SIGNED
....../....../.......	:	MALE.................☐ FEMALE.............☐	REASON: COMMENTS:	YES: ☐ NO: ☐	STAFF NAME: SIGNED:

DATE	TIME	PERSON REFUSED	PRODUCT/COMMENTS	AGED FOR ID	REFUSED BY/SIGNED
....../....../.......	:	MALE.................☐ FEMALE.............☐	REASON: COMMENTS:	YES: ☐ NO: ☐	STAFF NAME: SIGNED:

DATE	TIME	PERSON REFUSED	PRODUCT/COMMENTS	AGED FOR ID	REFUSED BY/SIGNED
....../....../.......	:	MALE.................☐ FEMALE.............☐	REASON: COMMENTS:	YES: ☐ NO: ☐	STAFF NAME: SIGNED:

CHALLENGE 25
Records of refusals

DATE	TIME	PERSON REFUSED	PRODUCT/COMMENTS	AGED FOR ID	REFUSED BY/SIGNED
....../....../.......	:	MALE................. ☐ FEMALE.............. ☐	REASON: COMMENTS:	YES: ☐ NO: ☐	STAFF NAME: SIGNED:

DATE	TIME	PERSON REFUSED	PRODUCT/COMMENTS	AGED FOR ID	REFUSED BY/SIGNED
....../....../.......	:	MALE................. ☐ FEMALE.............. ☐	REASON: COMMENTS:	YES: ☐ NO: ☐	STAFF NAME: SIGNED:

DATE	TIME	PERSON REFUSED	PRODUCT/COMMENTS	AGED FOR ID	REFUSED BY/SIGNED
....../....../.......	:	MALE................. ☐ FEMALE.............. ☐	REASON: COMMENTS:	YES: ☐ NO: ☐	STAFF NAME: SIGNED:

DATE	TIME	PERSON REFUSED	PRODUCT/COMMENTS	AGED FOR ID	REFUSED BY/SIGNED
....../....../.......	:	MALE................. ☐ FEMALE.............. ☐	REASON: COMMENTS:	YES: ☐ NO: ☐	STAFF NAME: SIGNED:

DATE	TIME	PERSON REFUSED	PRODUCT/COMMENTS	AGED FOR ID	REFUSED BY/SIGNED
....../....../.......	:	MALE................. ☐ FEMALE.............. ☐	REASON: COMMENTS:	YES: ☐ NO: ☐	STAFF NAME: SIGNED:

DATE	TIME	PERSON REFUSED	PRODUCT/COMMENTS	AGED FOR ID	REFUSED BY/SIGNED
....../....../.......	:	MALE................. ☐ FEMALE.............. ☐	REASON: COMMENTS:	YES: ☐ NO: ☐	STAFF NAME: SIGNED:

CHALLENGE 25
Records of refusals

DATE	TIME	PERSON REFUSED	PRODUCT/COMMENTS	AGED FOR ID	REFUSED BY/SIGNED
....../....../......	:	MALE................ ☐ FEMALE.............. ☐	REASON: COMMENTS:	YES: ☐ NO: ☐	STAFF NAME: SIGNED:

DATE	TIME	PERSON REFUSED	PRODUCT/COMMENTS	AGED FOR ID	REFUSED BY/SIGNED
....../....../......	:	MALE................ ☐ FEMALE.............. ☐	REASON: COMMENTS:	YES: ☐ NO: ☐	STAFF NAME: SIGNED:

DATE	TIME	PERSON REFUSED	PRODUCT/COMMENTS	AGED FOR ID	REFUSED BY/SIGNED
....../....../......	:	MALE................ ☐ FEMALE.............. ☐	REASON: COMMENTS:	YES: ☐ NO: ☐	STAFF NAME: SIGNED:

DATE	TIME	PERSON REFUSED	PRODUCT/COMMENTS	AGED FOR ID	REFUSED BY/SIGNED
....../....../......	:	MALE................ ☐ FEMALE.............. ☐	REASON: COMMENTS:	YES: ☐ NO: ☐	STAFF NAME: SIGNED:

DATE	TIME	PERSON REFUSED	PRODUCT/COMMENTS	AGED FOR ID	REFUSED BY/SIGNED
....../....../......	:	MALE................ ☐ FEMALE.............. ☐	REASON: COMMENTS:	YES: ☐ NO: ☐	STAFF NAME: SIGNED:

DATE	TIME	PERSON REFUSED	PRODUCT/COMMENTS	AGED FOR ID	REFUSED BY/SIGNED
....../....../......	:	MALE................ ☐ FEMALE.............. ☐	REASON: COMMENTS:	YES: ☐ NO: ☐	STAFF NAME: SIGNED:

CHALLENGE 25
Records of refusals

DATE	TIME	PERSON REFUSED	PRODUCT/COMMENTS	AGED FOR ID	REFUSED BY/SIGNED
....../....../......	:	MALE.................☐ FEMALE..............☐	REASON: COMMENTS:	YES: ☐ NO: ☐	STAFF NAME: SIGNED:

DATE	TIME	PERSON REFUSED	PRODUCT/COMMENTS	AGED FOR ID	REFUSED BY/SIGNED
....../....../......	:	MALE.................☐ FEMALE..............☐	REASON: COMMENTS:	YES: ☐ NO: ☐	STAFF NAME: SIGNED:

DATE	TIME	PERSON REFUSED	PRODUCT/COMMENTS	AGED FOR ID	REFUSED BY/SIGNED
....../....../......	:	MALE.................☐ FEMALE..............☐	REASON: COMMENTS:	YES: ☐ NO: ☐	STAFF NAME: SIGNED:

DATE	TIME	PERSON REFUSED	PRODUCT/COMMENTS	AGED FOR ID	REFUSED BY/SIGNED
....../....../......	:	MALE.................☐ FEMALE..............☐	REASON: COMMENTS:	YES: ☐ NO: ☐	STAFF NAME: SIGNED:

DATE	TIME	PERSON REFUSED	PRODUCT/COMMENTS	AGED FOR ID	REFUSED BY/SIGNED
....../....../......	:	MALE.................☐ FEMALE..............☐	REASON: COMMENTS:	YES: ☐ NO: ☐	STAFF NAME: SIGNED:

DATE	TIME	PERSON REFUSED	PRODUCT/COMMENTS	AGED FOR ID	REFUSED BY/SIGNED
....../....../......	:	MALE.................☐ FEMALE..............☐	REASON: COMMENTS:	YES: ☐ NO: ☐	STAFF NAME: SIGNED:

CHALLENGE 25
Records of refusals

DATE	TIME	PERSON REFUSED	PRODUCT/COMMENTS	AGED FOR ID	REFUSED BY/SIGNED
....../....../......	:	MALE...................☐ FEMALE...............☐	REASON: COMMENTS:	YES: ☐ NO: ☐	STAFF NAME: SIGNED:

DATE	TIME	PERSON REFUSED	PRODUCT/COMMENTS	AGED FOR ID	REFUSED BY/SIGNED
....../....../......	:	MALE...................☐ FEMALE...............☐	REASON: COMMENTS:	YES: ☐ NO: ☐	STAFF NAME: SIGNED:

DATE	TIME	PERSON REFUSED	PRODUCT/COMMENTS	AGED FOR ID	REFUSED BY/SIGNED
....../....../......	:	MALE...................☐ FEMALE...............☐	REASON: COMMENTS:	YES: ☐ NO: ☐	STAFF NAME: SIGNED:

DATE	TIME	PERSON REFUSED	PRODUCT/COMMENTS	AGED FOR ID	REFUSED BY/SIGNED
....../....../......	:	MALE...................☐ FEMALE...............☐	REASON: COMMENTS:	YES: ☐ NO: ☐	STAFF NAME: SIGNED:

DATE	TIME	PERSON REFUSED	PRODUCT/COMMENTS	AGED FOR ID	REFUSED BY/SIGNED
....../....../......	:	MALE...................☐ FEMALE...............☐	REASON: COMMENTS:	YES: ☐ NO: ☐	STAFF NAME: SIGNED:

DATE	TIME	PERSON REFUSED	PRODUCT/COMMENTS	AGED FOR ID	REFUSED BY/SIGNED
....../....../......	:	MALE...................☐ FEMALE...............☐	REASON: COMMENTS:	YES: ☐ NO: ☐	STAFF NAME: SIGNED:

CHALLENGE 25
Records of refusals

DATE	TIME	PERSON REFUSED	PRODUCT/COMMENTS	AGED FOR ID	REFUSED BY/SIGNED
....../....../......	:	MALE.................☐ FEMALE.............☐	REASON: COMMENTS:	YES: ☐ NO: ☐	STAFF NAME: SIGNED:

DATE	TIME	PERSON REFUSED	PRODUCT/COMMENTS	AGED FOR ID	REFUSED BY/SIGNED
....../....../......	:	MALE.................☐ FEMALE.............☐	REASON: COMMENTS:	YES: ☐ NO: ☐	STAFF NAME: SIGNED:

DATE	TIME	PERSON REFUSED	PRODUCT/COMMENTS	AGED FOR ID	REFUSED BY/SIGNED
....../....../......	:	MALE.................☐ FEMALE.............☐	REASON: COMMENTS:	YES: ☐ NO: ☐	STAFF NAME: SIGNED:

DATE	TIME	PERSON REFUSED	PRODUCT/COMMENTS	AGED FOR ID	REFUSED BY/SIGNED
....../....../......	:	MALE.................☐ FEMALE.............☐	REASON: COMMENTS:	YES: ☐ NO: ☐	STAFF NAME: SIGNED:

DATE	TIME	PERSON REFUSED	PRODUCT/COMMENTS	AGED FOR ID	REFUSED BY/SIGNED
....../....../......	:	MALE.................☐ FEMALE.............☐	REASON: COMMENTS:	YES: ☐ NO: ☐	STAFF NAME: SIGNED:

DATE	TIME	PERSON REFUSED	PRODUCT/COMMENTS	AGED FOR ID	REFUSED BY/SIGNED
....../....../......	:	MALE.................☐ FEMALE.............☐	REASON: COMMENTS:	YES: ☐ NO: ☐	STAFF NAME: SIGNED:

CHALLENGE 25
Records of refusals

DATE	TIME	PERSON REFUSED	PRODUCT/COMMENTS	AGED FOR ID	REFUSED BY/SIGNED
....../....../......	:	MALE.................. ☐ FEMALE.............. ☐	REASON: COMMENTS:	YES: ☐ NO: ☐	STAFF NAME: SIGNED:

DATE	TIME	PERSON REFUSED	PRODUCT/COMMENTS	AGED FOR ID	REFUSED BY/SIGNED
....../....../......	:	MALE.................. ☐ FEMALE.............. ☐	REASON: COMMENTS:	YES: ☐ NO: ☐	STAFF NAME: SIGNED:

DATE	TIME	PERSON REFUSED	PRODUCT/COMMENTS	AGED FOR ID	REFUSED BY/SIGNED
....../....../......	:	MALE.................. ☐ FEMALE.............. ☐	REASON: COMMENTS:	YES: ☐ NO: ☐	STAFF NAME: SIGNED:

DATE	TIME	PERSON REFUSED	PRODUCT/COMMENTS	AGED FOR ID	REFUSED BY/SIGNED
....../....../......	:	MALE.................. ☐ FEMALE.............. ☐	REASON: COMMENTS:	YES: ☐ NO: ☐	STAFF NAME: SIGNED:

DATE	TIME	PERSON REFUSED	PRODUCT/COMMENTS	AGED FOR ID	REFUSED BY/SIGNED
....../....../......	:	MALE.................. ☐ FEMALE.............. ☐	REASON: COMMENTS:	YES: ☐ NO: ☐	STAFF NAME: SIGNED:

DATE	TIME	PERSON REFUSED	PRODUCT/COMMENTS	AGED FOR ID	REFUSED BY/SIGNED
....../....../......	:	MALE.................. ☐ FEMALE.............. ☐	REASON: COMMENTS:	YES: ☐ NO: ☐	STAFF NAME: SIGNED:

CHALLENGE 25
Records of refusals

DATE	TIME	PERSON REFUSED	PRODUCT/COMMENTS	AGED FOR ID	REFUSED BY/SIGNED
....../....../......	:	MALE................☐ FEMALE............☐	REASON: COMMENTS:	YES: ☐ NO: ☐	STAFF NAME: SIGNED:

DATE	TIME	PERSON REFUSED	PRODUCT/COMMENTS	AGED FOR ID	REFUSED BY/SIGNED
....../....../......	:	MALE................☐ FEMALE............☐	REASON: COMMENTS:	YES: ☐ NO: ☐	STAFF NAME: SIGNED:

DATE	TIME	PERSON REFUSED	PRODUCT/COMMENTS	AGED FOR ID	REFUSED BY/SIGNED
....../....../......	:	MALE................☐ FEMALE............☐	REASON: COMMENTS:	YES: ☐ NO: ☐	STAFF NAME: SIGNED:

DATE	TIME	PERSON REFUSED	PRODUCT/COMMENTS	AGED FOR ID	REFUSED BY/SIGNED
....../....../......	:	MALE................☐ FEMALE............☐	REASON: COMMENTS:	YES: ☐ NO: ☐	STAFF NAME: SIGNED:

DATE	TIME	PERSON REFUSED	PRODUCT/COMMENTS	AGED FOR ID	REFUSED BY/SIGNED
....../....../......	:	MALE................☐ FEMALE............☐	REASON: COMMENTS:	YES: ☐ NO: ☐	STAFF NAME: SIGNED:

DATE	TIME	PERSON REFUSED	PRODUCT/COMMENTS	AGED FOR ID	REFUSED BY/SIGNED
....../....../......	:	MALE................☐ FEMALE............☐	REASON: COMMENTS:	YES: ☐ NO: ☐	STAFF NAME: SIGNED:

CHALLENGE 25
Records of refusals

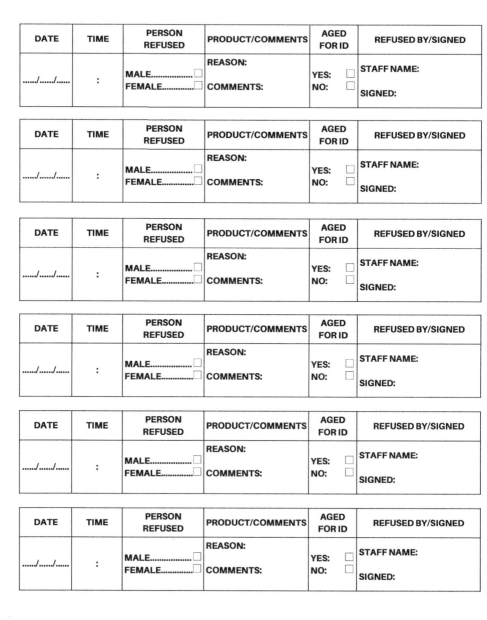

DATE	TIME	PERSON REFUSED	PRODUCT/COMMENTS	AGED FOR ID	REFUSED BY/SIGNED
....../....../......	:	MALE................☐ FEMALE...............☐	REASON: COMMENTS:	YES: ☐ NO: ☐	STAFF NAME: SIGNED:

DATE	TIME	PERSON REFUSED	PRODUCT/COMMENTS	AGED FOR ID	REFUSED BY/SIGNED
....../....../......	:	MALE................☐ FEMALE...............☐	REASON: COMMENTS:	YES: ☐ NO: ☐	STAFF NAME: SIGNED:

DATE	TIME	PERSON REFUSED	PRODUCT/COMMENTS	AGED FOR ID	REFUSED BY/SIGNED
....../....../......	:	MALE................☐ FEMALE...............☐	REASON: COMMENTS:	YES: ☐ NO: ☐	STAFF NAME: SIGNED:

DATE	TIME	PERSON REFUSED	PRODUCT/COMMENTS	AGED FOR ID	REFUSED BY/SIGNED
....../....../......	:	MALE................☐ FEMALE...............☐	REASON: COMMENTS:	YES: ☐ NO: ☐	STAFF NAME: SIGNED:

DATE	TIME	PERSON REFUSED	PRODUCT/COMMENTS	AGED FOR ID	REFUSED BY/SIGNED
....../....../......	:	MALE................☐ FEMALE...............☐	REASON: COMMENTS:	YES: ☐ NO: ☐	STAFF NAME: SIGNED:

DATE	TIME	PERSON REFUSED	PRODUCT/COMMENTS	AGED FOR ID	REFUSED BY/SIGNED
....../....../......	:	MALE................☐ FEMALE...............☐	REASON: COMMENTS:	YES: ☐ NO: ☐	STAFF NAME: SIGNED:

CHALLENGE 25
Records of refusals

DATE	TIME	PERSON REFUSED	PRODUCT/COMMENTS	AGED FOR ID	REFUSED BY/SIGNED
...../ ....../	:	MALE.................☐ FEMALE.............☐	REASON: COMMENTS:	YES: ☐ NO: ☐	STAFF NAME: SIGNED:

DATE	TIME	PERSON REFUSED	PRODUCT/COMMENTS	AGED FOR ID	REFUSED BY/SIGNED
...../ ....../	:	MALE.................☐ FEMALE.............☐	REASON: COMMENTS:	YES: ☐ NO: ☐	STAFF NAME: SIGNED:

DATE	TIME	PERSON REFUSED	PRODUCT/COMMENTS	AGED FOR ID	REFUSED BY/SIGNED
...../ ....../	:	MALE.................☐ FEMALE.............☐	REASON: COMMENTS:	YES: ☐ NO: ☐	STAFF NAME: SIGNED:

DATE	TIME	PERSON REFUSED	PRODUCT/COMMENTS	AGED FOR ID	REFUSED BY/SIGNED
...../ ....../	:	MALE.................☐ FEMALE.............☐	REASON: COMMENTS:	YES: ☐ NO: ☐	STAFF NAME: SIGNED:

DATE	TIME	PERSON REFUSED	PRODUCT/COMMENTS	AGED FOR ID	REFUSED BY/SIGNED
...../ ....../	:	MALE.................☐ FEMALE.............☐	REASON: COMMENTS:	YES: ☐ NO: ☐	STAFF NAME: SIGNED:

DATE	TIME	PERSON REFUSED	PRODUCT/COMMENTS	AGED FOR ID	REFUSED BY/SIGNED
...../ ....../	:	MALE.................☐ FEMALE.............☐	REASON: COMMENTS:	YES: ☐ NO: ☐	STAFF NAME: SIGNED:

CHALLENGE 25
Records of refusals

DATE	TIME	PERSON REFUSED	PRODUCT/COMMENTS	AGED FOR ID	REFUSED BY/SIGNED
....../....../......	:	MALE................... ☐ FEMALE.............☐	REASON: COMMENTS:	YES: ☐ NO: ☐	STAFF NAME: SIGNED:

DATE	TIME	PERSON REFUSED	PRODUCT/COMMENTS	AGED FOR ID	REFUSED BY/SIGNED
....../....../......	:	MALE................... ☐ FEMALE.............☐	REASON: COMMENTS:	YES: ☐ NO: ☐	STAFF NAME: SIGNED:

DATE	TIME	PERSON REFUSED	PRODUCT/COMMENTS	AGED FOR ID	REFUSED BY/SIGNED
....../....../......	:	MALE................... ☐ FEMALE.............☐	REASON: COMMENTS:	YES: ☐ NO: ☐	STAFF NAME: SIGNED:

DATE	TIME	PERSON REFUSED	PRODUCT/COMMENTS	AGED FOR ID	REFUSED BY/SIGNED
....../....../......	:	MALE................... ☐ FEMALE.............☐	REASON: COMMENTS:	YES: ☐ NO: ☐	STAFF NAME: SIGNED:

DATE	TIME	PERSON REFUSED	PRODUCT/COMMENTS	AGED FOR ID	REFUSED BY/SIGNED
....../....../......	:	MALE................... ☐ FEMALE.............☐	REASON: COMMENTS:	YES: ☐ NO: ☐	STAFF NAME: SIGNED:

DATE	TIME	PERSON REFUSED	PRODUCT/COMMENTS	AGED FOR ID	REFUSED BY/SIGNED
....../....../......	:	MALE................... ☐ FEMALE.............☐	REASON: COMMENTS:	YES: ☐ NO: ☐	STAFF NAME: SIGNED:

CHALLENGE 25
Records of refusals

DATE	TIME	PERSON REFUSED	PRODUCT/COMMENTS	AGED FOR ID	REFUSED BY/SIGNED
....../ ....../	:	MALE................☐ FEMALE..............☐	REASON: COMMENTS:	YES: ☐ NO: ☐	STAFF NAME: SIGNED:

DATE	TIME	PERSON REFUSED	PRODUCT/COMMENTS	AGED FOR ID	REFUSED BY/SIGNED
....../ ....../	:	MALE................☐ FEMALE..............☐	REASON: COMMENTS:	YES: ☐ NO: ☐	STAFF NAME: SIGNED:

DATE	TIME	PERSON REFUSED	PRODUCT/COMMENTS	AGED FOR ID	REFUSED BY/SIGNED
....../ ....../	:	MALE................☐ FEMALE..............☐	REASON: COMMENTS:	YES: ☐ NO: ☐	STAFF NAME: SIGNED:

DATE	TIME	PERSON REFUSED	PRODUCT/COMMENTS	AGED FOR ID	REFUSED BY/SIGNED
....../ ....../	:	MALE................☐ FEMALE..............☐	REASON: COMMENTS:	YES: ☐ NO: ☐	STAFF NAME: SIGNED:

DATE	TIME	PERSON REFUSED	PRODUCT/COMMENTS	AGED FOR ID	REFUSED BY/SIGNED
....../ ....../	:	MALE................☐ FEMALE..............☐	REASON: COMMENTS:	YES: ☐ NO: ☐	STAFF NAME: SIGNED:

DATE	TIME	PERSON REFUSED	PRODUCT/COMMENTS	AGED FOR ID	REFUSED BY/SIGNED
....../ ....../	:	MALE................☐ FEMALE..............☐	REASON: COMMENTS:	YES: ☐ NO: ☐	STAFF NAME: SIGNED:

CHALLENGE 25
Records of refusals

🚫18

DATE	TIME	PERSON REFUSED	PRODUCT/COMMENTS	AGED FOR ID	REFUSED BY/SIGNED
....../....../......	:	MALE................ ☐ FEMALE............. ☐	REASON: COMMENTS:	YES: ☐ NO: ☐	STAFF NAME: SIGNED:

DATE	TIME	PERSON REFUSED	PRODUCT/COMMENTS	AGED FOR ID	REFUSED BY/SIGNED
....../....../......	:	MALE................ ☐ FEMALE............. ☐	REASON: COMMENTS:	YES: ☐ NO: ☐	STAFF NAME: SIGNED:

DATE	TIME	PERSON REFUSED	PRODUCT/COMMENTS	AGED FOR ID	REFUSED BY/SIGNED
....../....../......	:	MALE................ ☐ FEMALE............. ☐	REASON: COMMENTS:	YES: ☐ NO: ☐	STAFF NAME: SIGNED:

DATE	TIME	PERSON REFUSED	PRODUCT/COMMENTS	AGED FOR ID	REFUSED BY/SIGNED
....../....../......	:	MALE................ ☐ FEMALE............. ☐	REASON: COMMENTS:	YES: ☐ NO: ☐	STAFF NAME: SIGNED:

DATE	TIME	PERSON REFUSED	PRODUCT/COMMENTS	AGED FOR ID	REFUSED BY/SIGNED
....../....../......	:	MALE................ ☐ FEMALE............. ☐	REASON: COMMENTS:	YES: ☐ NO: ☐	STAFF NAME: SIGNED:

DATE	TIME	PERSON REFUSED	PRODUCT/COMMENTS	AGED FOR ID	REFUSED BY/SIGNED
....../....../......	:	MALE................ ☐ FEMALE............. ☐	REASON: COMMENTS:	YES: ☐ NO: ☐	STAFF NAME: SIGNED:

CHALLENGE 25
Records of refusals

DATE	TIME	PERSON REFUSED	PRODUCT/COMMENTS	AGED FOR ID	REFUSED BY/SIGNED
....../ ....../	:	MALE.................☐ FEMALE.............☐	REASON: COMMENTS:	YES: ☐ NO: ☐	STAFF NAME: SIGNED:

DATE	TIME	PERSON REFUSED	PRODUCT/COMMENTS	AGED FOR ID	REFUSED BY/SIGNED
....../ ....../	:	MALE.................☐ FEMALE.............☐	REASON: COMMENTS:	YES: ☐ NO: ☐	STAFF NAME: SIGNED:

DATE	TIME	PERSON REFUSED	PRODUCT/COMMENTS	AGED FOR ID	REFUSED BY/SIGNED
....../ ....../	:	MALE.................☐ FEMALE.............☐	REASON: COMMENTS:	YES: ☐ NO: ☐	STAFF NAME: SIGNED:

DATE	TIME	PERSON REFUSED	PRODUCT/COMMENTS	AGED FOR ID	REFUSED BY/SIGNED
....../ ....../	:	MALE.................☐ FEMALE.............☐	REASON: COMMENTS:	YES: ☐ NO: ☐	STAFF NAME: SIGNED:

DATE	TIME	PERSON REFUSED	PRODUCT/COMMENTS	AGED FOR ID	REFUSED BY/SIGNED
....../ ....../	:	MALE.................☐ FEMALE.............☐	REASON: COMMENTS:	YES: ☐ NO: ☐	STAFF NAME: SIGNED:

DATE	TIME	PERSON REFUSED	PRODUCT/COMMENTS	AGED FOR ID	REFUSED BY/SIGNED
....../ ....../	:	MALE.................☐ FEMALE.............☐	REASON: COMMENTS:	YES: ☐ NO: ☐	STAFF NAME: SIGNED:

CHALLENGE 25
Records of refusals

DATE	TIME	PERSON REFUSED	PRODUCT/COMMENTS	AGED FOR ID	REFUSED BY/SIGNED
....../....../......	:	MALE.................. ☐ FEMALE.............. ☐	REASON: COMMENTS:	YES: ☐ NO: ☐	STAFF NAME: SIGNED:

DATE	TIME	PERSON REFUSED	PRODUCT/COMMENTS	AGED FOR ID	REFUSED BY/SIGNED
....../....../......	:	MALE.................. ☐ FEMALE.............. ☐	REASON: COMMENTS:	YES: ☐ NO: ☐	STAFF NAME: SIGNED:

DATE	TIME	PERSON REFUSED	PRODUCT/COMMENTS	AGED FOR ID	REFUSED BY/SIGNED
....../....../......	:	MALE.................. ☐ FEMALE.............. ☐	REASON: COMMENTS:	YES: ☐ NO: ☐	STAFF NAME: SIGNED:

DATE	TIME	PERSON REFUSED	PRODUCT/COMMENTS	AGED FOR ID	REFUSED BY/SIGNED
....../....../......	:	MALE.................. ☐ FEMALE.............. ☐	REASON: COMMENTS:	YES: ☐ NO: ☐	STAFF NAME: SIGNED:

DATE	TIME	PERSON REFUSED	PRODUCT/COMMENTS	AGED FOR ID	REFUSED BY/SIGNED
....../....../......	:	MALE.................. ☐ FEMALE.............. ☐	REASON: COMMENTS:	YES: ☐ NO: ☐	STAFF NAME: SIGNED:

DATE	TIME	PERSON REFUSED	PRODUCT/COMMENTS	AGED FOR ID	REFUSED BY/SIGNED
....../....../......	:	MALE.................. ☐ FEMALE.............. ☐	REASON: COMMENTS:	YES: ☐ NO: ☐	STAFF NAME: SIGNED:

CHALLENGE 25
Records of refusals

DATE	TIME	PERSON REFUSED	PRODUCT/COMMENTS	AGED FOR ID	REFUSED BY/SIGNED
....../....../......	:	MALE...................☐ FEMALE..............☐	REASON: COMMENTS:	YES: ☐ NO: ☐	STAFF NAME: SIGNED:

DATE	TIME	PERSON REFUSED	PRODUCT/COMMENTS	AGED FOR ID	REFUSED BY/SIGNED
....../....../......	:	MALE...................☐ FEMALE..............☐	REASON: COMMENTS:	YES: ☐ NO: ☐	STAFF NAME: SIGNED:

DATE	TIME	PERSON REFUSED	PRODUCT/COMMENTS	AGED FOR ID	REFUSED BY/SIGNED
....../....../......	:	MALE...................☐ FEMALE..............☐	REASON: COMMENTS:	YES: ☐ NO: ☐	STAFF NAME: SIGNED:

DATE	TIME	PERSON REFUSED	PRODUCT/COMMENTS	AGED FOR ID	REFUSED BY/SIGNED
....../....../......	:	MALE...................☐ FEMALE..............☐	REASON: COMMENTS:	YES: ☐ NO: ☐	STAFF NAME: SIGNED:

DATE	TIME	PERSON REFUSED	PRODUCT/COMMENTS	AGED FOR ID	REFUSED BY/SIGNED
....../....../......	:	MALE...................☐ FEMALE..............☐	REASON: COMMENTS:	YES: ☐ NO: ☐	STAFF NAME: SIGNED:

DATE	TIME	PERSON REFUSED	PRODUCT/COMMENTS	AGED FOR ID	REFUSED BY/SIGNED
....../....../......	:	MALE...................☐ FEMALE..............☐	REASON: COMMENTS:	YES: ☐ NO: ☐	STAFF NAME: SIGNED:

CHALLENGE 25
Records of refusals

DATE	TIME	PERSON REFUSED	PRODUCT/COMMENTS	AGED FOR ID	REFUSED BY/SIGNED
....../....../......	:	MALE.................. ☐ FEMALE.............☐	REASON: COMMENTS:	YES: ☐ NO: ☐	STAFF NAME: SIGNED:

DATE	TIME	PERSON REFUSED	PRODUCT/COMMENTS	AGED FOR ID	REFUSED BY/SIGNED
....../....../......	:	MALE.................. ☐ FEMALE.............☐	REASON: COMMENTS:	YES: ☐ NO: ☐	STAFF NAME: SIGNED:

DATE	TIME	PERSON REFUSED	PRODUCT/COMMENTS	AGED FOR ID	REFUSED BY/SIGNED
....../....../......	:	MALE.................. ☐ FEMALE.............☐	REASON: COMMENTS:	YES: ☐ NO: ☐	STAFF NAME: SIGNED:

DATE	TIME	PERSON REFUSED	PRODUCT/COMMENTS	AGED FOR ID	REFUSED BY/SIGNED
....../....../......	:	MALE.................. ☐ FEMALE.............☐	REASON: COMMENTS:	YES: ☐ NO: ☐	STAFF NAME: SIGNED:

DATE	TIME	PERSON REFUSED	PRODUCT/COMMENTS	AGED FOR ID	REFUSED BY/SIGNED
....../....../......	:	MALE.................. ☐ FEMALE.............☐	REASON: COMMENTS:	YES: ☐ NO: ☐	STAFF NAME: SIGNED:

DATE	TIME	PERSON REFUSED	PRODUCT/COMMENTS	AGED FOR ID	REFUSED BY/SIGNED
....../....../......	:	MALE.................. ☐ FEMALE.............☐	REASON: COMMENTS:	YES: ☐ NO: ☐	STAFF NAME: SIGNED:

CHALLENGE 25
Records of refusals

DATE	TIME	PERSON REFUSED	PRODUCT/COMMENTS	AGED FOR ID	REFUSED BY/SIGNED
....../....../......	:	MALE................☐ FEMALE............☐	REASON: COMMENTS:	YES: ☐ NO: ☐	STAFF NAME: SIGNED:

DATE	TIME	PERSON REFUSED	PRODUCT/COMMENTS	AGED FOR ID	REFUSED BY/SIGNED
....../....../......	:	MALE................☐ FEMALE............☐	REASON: COMMENTS:	YES: ☐ NO: ☐	STAFF NAME: SIGNED:

DATE	TIME	PERSON REFUSED	PRODUCT/COMMENTS	AGED FOR ID	REFUSED BY/SIGNED
....../....../......	:	MALE................☐ FEMALE............☐	REASON: COMMENTS:	YES: ☐ NO: ☐	STAFF NAME: SIGNED:

DATE	TIME	PERSON REFUSED	PRODUCT/COMMENTS	AGED FOR ID	REFUSED BY/SIGNED
....../....../......	:	MALE................☐ FEMALE............☐	REASON: COMMENTS:	YES: ☐ NO: ☐	STAFF NAME: SIGNED:

DATE	TIME	PERSON REFUSED	PRODUCT/COMMENTS	AGED FOR ID	REFUSED BY/SIGNED
....../....../......	:	MALE................☐ FEMALE............☐	REASON: COMMENTS:	YES: ☐ NO: ☐	STAFF NAME: SIGNED:

DATE	TIME	PERSON REFUSED	PRODUCT/COMMENTS	AGED FOR ID	REFUSED BY/SIGNED
....../....../......	:	MALE................☐ FEMALE............☐	REASON: COMMENTS:	YES: ☐ NO: ☐	STAFF NAME: SIGNED:

CHALLENGE 25
Records of refusals

🚫18

DATE	TIME	PERSON REFUSED	PRODUCT/COMMENTS	AGED FOR ID	REFUSED BY/SIGNED
....../....../......	:	MALE...................☐ FEMALE...............☐	REASON: COMMENTS:	YES: ☐ NO: ☐	STAFF NAME: SIGNED:

DATE	TIME	PERSON REFUSED	PRODUCT/COMMENTS	AGED FOR ID	REFUSED BY/SIGNED
....../....../......	:	MALE...................☐ FEMALE...............☐	REASON: COMMENTS:	YES: ☐ NO: ☐	STAFF NAME: SIGNED:

DATE	TIME	PERSON REFUSED	PRODUCT/COMMENTS	AGED FOR ID	REFUSED BY/SIGNED
....../....../......	:	MALE...................☐ FEMALE...............☐	REASON: COMMENTS:	YES: ☐ NO: ☐	STAFF NAME: SIGNED:

DATE	TIME	PERSON REFUSED	PRODUCT/COMMENTS	AGED FOR ID	REFUSED BY/SIGNED
....../....../......	:	MALE...................☐ FEMALE...............☐	REASON: COMMENTS:	YES: ☐ NO: ☐	STAFF NAME: SIGNED:

DATE	TIME	PERSON REFUSED	PRODUCT/COMMENTS	AGED FOR ID	REFUSED BY/SIGNED
....../....../......	:	MALE...................☐ FEMALE...............☐	REASON: COMMENTS:	YES: ☐ NO: ☐	STAFF NAME: SIGNED:

DATE	TIME	PERSON REFUSED	PRODUCT/COMMENTS	AGED FOR ID	REFUSED BY/SIGNED
....../....../......	:	MALE...................☐ FEMALE...............☐	REASON: COMMENTS:	YES: ☐ NO: ☐	STAFF NAME: SIGNED:

CHALLENGE 25
Records of refusals

DATE	TIME	PERSON REFUSED	PRODUCT/COMMENTS	AGED FOR ID	REFUSED BY/SIGNED
....../....../......	:	MALE..................☐ FEMALE..............☐	REASON: COMMENTS:	YES: ☐ NO: ☐	STAFF NAME: SIGNED:

DATE	TIME	PERSON REFUSED	PRODUCT/COMMENTS	AGED FOR ID	REFUSED BY/SIGNED
....../....../......	:	MALE..................☐ FEMALE..............☐	REASON: COMMENTS:	YES: ☐ NO: ☐	STAFF NAME: SIGNED:

DATE	TIME	PERSON REFUSED	PRODUCT/COMMENTS	AGED FOR ID	REFUSED BY/SIGNED
....../....../......	:	MALE..................☐ FEMALE..............☐	REASON: COMMENTS:	YES: ☐ NO: ☐	STAFF NAME: SIGNED:

DATE	TIME	PERSON REFUSED	PRODUCT/COMMENTS	AGED FOR ID	REFUSED BY/SIGNED
....../....../......	:	MALE..................☐ FEMALE..............☐	REASON: COMMENTS:	YES: ☐ NO: ☐	STAFF NAME: SIGNED:

DATE	TIME	PERSON REFUSED	PRODUCT/COMMENTS	AGED FOR ID	REFUSED BY/SIGNED
....../....../......	:	MALE..................☐ FEMALE..............☐	REASON: COMMENTS:	YES: ☐ NO: ☐	STAFF NAME: SIGNED:

DATE	TIME	PERSON REFUSED	PRODUCT/COMMENTS	AGED FOR ID	REFUSED BY/SIGNED
....../....../......	:	MALE..................☐ FEMALE..............☐	REASON: COMMENTS:	YES: ☐ NO: ☐	STAFF NAME: SIGNED:

CHALLENGE 25
Records of refusals

DATE	TIME	PERSON REFUSED	PRODUCT/COMMENTS	AGED FOR ID	REFUSED BY/SIGNED
....../....../......	:	MALE.................☐ FEMALE..............☐	REASON: COMMENTS:	YES: ☐ NO: ☐	STAFF NAME: SIGNED:

DATE	TIME	PERSON REFUSED	PRODUCT/COMMENTS	AGED FOR ID	REFUSED BY/SIGNED
....../....../......	:	MALE.................☐ FEMALE..............☐	REASON: COMMENTS:	YES: ☐ NO: ☐	STAFF NAME: SIGNED:

DATE	TIME	PERSON REFUSED	PRODUCT/COMMENTS	AGED FOR ID	REFUSED BY/SIGNED
....../....../......	:	MALE.................☐ FEMALE..............☐	REASON: COMMENTS:	YES: ☐ NO: ☐	STAFF NAME: SIGNED:

DATE	TIME	PERSON REFUSED	PRODUCT/COMMENTS	AGED FOR ID	REFUSED BY/SIGNED
....../....../......	:	MALE.................☐ FEMALE..............☐	REASON: COMMENTS:	YES: ☐ NO: ☐	STAFF NAME: SIGNED:

DATE	TIME	PERSON REFUSED	PRODUCT/COMMENTS	AGED FOR ID	REFUSED BY/SIGNED
....../....../......	:	MALE.................☐ FEMALE..............☐	REASON: COMMENTS:	YES: ☐ NO: ☐	STAFF NAME: SIGNED:

DATE	TIME	PERSON REFUSED	PRODUCT/COMMENTS	AGED FOR ID	REFUSED BY/SIGNED
....../....../......	:	MALE.................☐ FEMALE..............☐	REASON: COMMENTS:	YES: ☐ NO: ☐	STAFF NAME: SIGNED:

CHALLENGE 25
Records of refusals

DATE	TIME	PERSON REFUSED	PRODUCT/COMMENTS	AGED FOR ID	REFUSED BY/SIGNED
....../....../......	:	MALE.................☐ FEMALE.............☐	REASON: COMMENTS:	YES: ☐ NO: ☐	STAFF NAME: SIGNED:

DATE	TIME	PERSON REFUSED	PRODUCT/COMMENTS	AGED FOR ID	REFUSED BY/SIGNED
....../....../......	:	MALE.................☐ FEMALE.............☐	REASON: COMMENTS:	YES: ☐ NO: ☐	STAFF NAME: SIGNED:

DATE	TIME	PERSON REFUSED	PRODUCT/COMMENTS	AGED FOR ID	REFUSED BY/SIGNED
....../....../......	:	MALE.................☐ FEMALE.............☐	REASON: COMMENTS:	YES: ☐ NO: ☐	STAFF NAME: SIGNED:

DATE	TIME	PERSON REFUSED	PRODUCT/COMMENTS	AGED FOR ID	REFUSED BY/SIGNED
....../....../......	:	MALE.................☐ FEMALE.............☐	REASON: COMMENTS:	YES: ☐ NO: ☐	STAFF NAME: SIGNED:

DATE	TIME	PERSON REFUSED	PRODUCT/COMMENTS	AGED FOR ID	REFUSED BY/SIGNED
....../....../......	:	MALE.................☐ FEMALE.............☐	REASON: COMMENTS:	YES: ☐ NO: ☐	STAFF NAME: SIGNED:

DATE	TIME	PERSON REFUSED	PRODUCT/COMMENTS	AGED FOR ID	REFUSED BY/SIGNED
....../....../......	:	MALE.................☐ FEMALE.............☐	REASON: COMMENTS:	YES: ☐ NO: ☐	STAFF NAME: SIGNED:

CHALLENGE 25
Records of refusals

DATE	TIME	PERSON REFUSED	PRODUCT/COMMENTS	AGED FOR ID	REFUSED BY/SIGNED
....../....../......	:	MALE................☐ FEMALE.............☐	REASON: COMMENTS:	YES: ☐ NO: ☐	STAFF NAME: SIGNED:

DATE	TIME	PERSON REFUSED	PRODUCT/COMMENTS	AGED FOR ID	REFUSED BY/SIGNED
....../....../......	:	MALE................☐ FEMALE.............☐	REASON: COMMENTS:	YES: ☐ NO: ☐	STAFF NAME: SIGNED:

DATE	TIME	PERSON REFUSED	PRODUCT/COMMENTS	AGED FOR ID	REFUSED BY/SIGNED
....../....../......	:	MALE................☐ FEMALE.............☐	REASON: COMMENTS:	YES: ☐ NO: ☐	STAFF NAME: SIGNED:

DATE	TIME	PERSON REFUSED	PRODUCT/COMMENTS	AGED FOR ID	REFUSED BY/SIGNED
....../....../......	:	MALE................☐ FEMALE.............☐	REASON: COMMENTS:	YES: ☐ NO: ☐	STAFF NAME: SIGNED:

DATE	TIME	PERSON REFUSED	PRODUCT/COMMENTS	AGED FOR ID	REFUSED BY/SIGNED
....../....../......	:	MALE................☐ FEMALE.............☐	REASON: COMMENTS:	YES: ☐ NO: ☐	STAFF NAME: SIGNED:

DATE	TIME	PERSON REFUSED	PRODUCT/COMMENTS	AGED FOR ID	REFUSED BY/SIGNED
....../....../......	:	MALE................☐ FEMALE.............☐	REASON: COMMENTS:	YES: ☐ NO: ☐	STAFF NAME: SIGNED:

CHALLENGE 25
Records of refusals

DATE	TIME	PERSON REFUSED	PRODUCT/COMMENTS	AGED FOR ID	REFUSED BY/SIGNED
....../ ....../	:	MALE..................☐ FEMALE..............☐	REASON: COMMENTS:	YES: ☐ NO: ☐	STAFF NAME: SIGNED:

DATE	TIME	PERSON REFUSED	PRODUCT/COMMENTS	AGED FOR ID	REFUSED BY/SIGNED
....../ ....../	:	MALE..................☐ FEMALE..............☐	REASON: COMMENTS:	YES: ☐ NO: ☐	STAFF NAME: SIGNED:

DATE	TIME	PERSON REFUSED	PRODUCT/COMMENTS	AGED FOR ID	REFUSED BY/SIGNED
....../ ....../	:	MALE..................☐ FEMALE..............☐	REASON: COMMENTS:	YES: ☐ NO: ☐	STAFF NAME: SIGNED:

DATE	TIME	PERSON REFUSED	PRODUCT/COMMENTS	AGED FOR ID	REFUSED BY/SIGNED
....../ ....../	:	MALE..................☐ FEMALE..............☐	REASON: COMMENTS:	YES: ☐ NO: ☐	STAFF NAME: SIGNED:

DATE	TIME	PERSON REFUSED	PRODUCT/COMMENTS	AGED FOR ID	REFUSED BY/SIGNED
....../ ....../	:	MALE..................☐ FEMALE..............☐	REASON: COMMENTS:	YES: ☐ NO: ☐	STAFF NAME: SIGNED:

DATE	TIME	PERSON REFUSED	PRODUCT/COMMENTS	AGED FOR ID	REFUSED BY/SIGNED
....../ ....../	:	MALE..................☐ FEMALE..............☐	REASON: COMMENTS:	YES: ☐ NO: ☐	STAFF NAME: SIGNED:

CHALLENGE 25
Records of refusals

DATE	TIME	PERSON REFUSED	PRODUCT/COMMENTS	AGED FOR ID	REFUSED BY/SIGNED
....../....../......	:	MALE................... ☐ FEMALE.............. ☐	REASON: COMMENTS:	YES: ☐ NO: ☐	STAFF NAME: SIGNED:

DATE	TIME	PERSON REFUSED	PRODUCT/COMMENTS	AGED FOR ID	REFUSED BY/SIGNED
....../....../......	:	MALE................... ☐ FEMALE.............. ☐	REASON: COMMENTS:	YES: ☐ NO: ☐	STAFF NAME: SIGNED:

DATE	TIME	PERSON REFUSED	PRODUCT/COMMENTS	AGED FOR ID	REFUSED BY/SIGNED
....../....../......	:	MALE................... ☐ FEMALE.............. ☐	REASON: COMMENTS:	YES: ☐ NO: ☐	STAFF NAME: SIGNED:

DATE	TIME	PERSON REFUSED	PRODUCT/COMMENTS	AGED FOR ID	REFUSED BY/SIGNED
....../....../......	:	MALE................... ☐ FEMALE.............. ☐	REASON: COMMENTS:	YES: ☐ NO: ☐	STAFF NAME: SIGNED:

DATE	TIME	PERSON REFUSED	PRODUCT/COMMENTS	AGED FOR ID	REFUSED BY/SIGNED
....../....../......	:	MALE................... ☐ FEMALE.............. ☐	REASON: COMMENTS:	YES: ☐ NO: ☐	STAFF NAME: SIGNED:

DATE	TIME	PERSON REFUSED	PRODUCT/COMMENTS	AGED FOR ID	REFUSED BY/SIGNED
....../....../......	:	MALE................... ☐ FEMALE.............. ☐	REASON: COMMENTS:	YES: ☐ NO: ☐	STAFF NAME: SIGNED:

CHALLENGE 25
Records of refusals

DATE	TIME	PERSON REFUSED	PRODUCT/COMMENTS	AGED FOR ID	REFUSED BY/SIGNED
....../....../......	:	MALE................. ☐ FEMALE.............. ☐	REASON: COMMENTS:	YES: ☐ NO: ☐	STAFF NAME: SIGNED:

DATE	TIME	PERSON REFUSED	PRODUCT/COMMENTS	AGED FOR ID	REFUSED BY/SIGNED
....../....../......	:	MALE................. ☐ FEMALE.............. ☐	REASON: COMMENTS:	YES: ☐ NO: ☐	STAFF NAME: SIGNED:

DATE	TIME	PERSON REFUSED	PRODUCT/COMMENTS	AGED FOR ID	REFUSED BY/SIGNED
....../....../......	:	MALE................. ☐ FEMALE.............. ☐	REASON: COMMENTS:	YES: ☐ NO: ☐	STAFF NAME: SIGNED:

DATE	TIME	PERSON REFUSED	PRODUCT/COMMENTS	AGED FOR ID	REFUSED BY/SIGNED
....../....../......	:	MALE................. ☐ FEMALE.............. ☐	REASON: COMMENTS:	YES: ☐ NO: ☐	STAFF NAME: SIGNED:

DATE	TIME	PERSON REFUSED	PRODUCT/COMMENTS	AGED FOR ID	REFUSED BY/SIGNED
....../....../......	:	MALE................. ☐ FEMALE.............. ☐	REASON: COMMENTS:	YES: ☐ NO: ☐	STAFF NAME: SIGNED:

DATE	TIME	PERSON REFUSED	PRODUCT/COMMENTS	AGED FOR ID	REFUSED BY/SIGNED
....../....../......	:	MALE................. ☐ FEMALE.............. ☐	REASON: COMMENTS:	YES: ☐ NO: ☐	STAFF NAME: SIGNED:

CHALLENGE 25
Records of refusals

🚫18

DATE	TIME	PERSON REFUSED	PRODUCT/COMMENTS	AGED FOR ID	REFUSED BY/SIGNED
....../....../......	:	MALE.................☐ FEMALE.............☐	REASON: COMMENTS:	YES: ☐ NO: ☐	STAFF NAME: SIGNED:

DATE	TIME	PERSON REFUSED	PRODUCT/COMMENTS	AGED FOR ID	REFUSED BY/SIGNED
....../....../......	:	MALE.................☐ FEMALE.............☐	REASON: COMMENTS:	YES: ☐ NO: ☐	STAFF NAME: SIGNED:

DATE	TIME	PERSON REFUSED	PRODUCT/COMMENTS	AGED FOR ID	REFUSED BY/SIGNED
....../....../......	:	MALE.................☐ FEMALE.............☐	REASON: COMMENTS:	YES: ☐ NO: ☐	STAFF NAME: SIGNED:

DATE	TIME	PERSON REFUSED	PRODUCT/COMMENTS	AGED FOR ID	REFUSED BY/SIGNED
....../....../......	:	MALE.................☐ FEMALE.............☐	REASON: COMMENTS:	YES: ☐ NO: ☐	STAFF NAME: SIGNED:

DATE	TIME	PERSON REFUSED	PRODUCT/COMMENTS	AGED FOR ID	REFUSED BY/SIGNED
....../....../......	:	MALE.................☐ FEMALE.............☐	REASON: COMMENTS:	YES: ☐ NO: ☐	STAFF NAME: SIGNED:

DATE	TIME	PERSON REFUSED	PRODUCT/COMMENTS	AGED FOR ID	REFUSED BY/SIGNED
....../....../......	:	MALE.................☐ FEMALE.............☐	REASON: COMMENTS:	YES: ☐ NO: ☐	STAFF NAME: SIGNED:

CHALLENGE 25
Records of refusals 🚫18

DATE	TIME	PERSON REFUSED	PRODUCT/COMMENTS	AGED FOR ID	REFUSED BY/SIGNED
....../....../.......	:	MALE..................☐ FEMALE..............☐	REASON: COMMENTS:	YES: ☐ NO: ☐	STAFF NAME: SIGNED:

DATE	TIME	PERSON REFUSED	PRODUCT/COMMENTS	AGED FOR ID	REFUSED BY/SIGNED
....../....../.......	:	MALE..................☐ FEMALE..............☐	REASON: COMMENTS:	YES: ☐ NO: ☐	STAFF NAME: SIGNED:

DATE	TIME	PERSON REFUSED	PRODUCT/COMMENTS	AGED FOR ID	REFUSED BY/SIGNED
....../....../.......	:	MALE..................☐ FEMALE..............☐	REASON: COMMENTS:	YES: ☐ NO: ☐	STAFF NAME: SIGNED:

DATE	TIME	PERSON REFUSED	PRODUCT/COMMENTS	AGED FOR ID	REFUSED BY/SIGNED
....../....../.......	:	MALE..................☐ FEMALE..............☐	REASON: COMMENTS:	YES: ☐ NO: ☐	STAFF NAME: SIGNED:

DATE	TIME	PERSON REFUSED	PRODUCT/COMMENTS	AGED FOR ID	REFUSED BY/SIGNED
....../....../.......	:	MALE..................☐ FEMALE..............☐	REASON: COMMENTS:	YES: ☐ NO: ☐	STAFF NAME: SIGNED:

DATE	TIME	PERSON REFUSED	PRODUCT/COMMENTS	AGED FOR ID	REFUSED BY/SIGNED
....../....../.......	:	MALE..................☐ FEMALE..............☐	REASON: COMMENTS:	YES: ☐ NO: ☐	STAFF NAME: SIGNED:

CHALLENGE 25
Records of refusals

DATE	TIME	PERSON REFUSED	PRODUCT/COMMENTS	AGED FOR ID	REFUSED BY/SIGNED
....../....../......	:	MALE................ ☐ FEMALE.............. ☐	REASON: COMMENTS:	YES: ☐ NO: ☐	STAFF NAME: SIGNED:

DATE	TIME	PERSON REFUSED	PRODUCT/COMMENTS	AGED FOR ID	REFUSED BY/SIGNED
....../....../......	:	MALE................ ☐ FEMALE.............. ☐	REASON: COMMENTS:	YES: ☐ NO: ☐	STAFF NAME: SIGNED:

DATE	TIME	PERSON REFUSED	PRODUCT/COMMENTS	AGED FOR ID	REFUSED BY/SIGNED
....../....../......	:	MALE................ ☐ FEMALE.............. ☐	REASON: COMMENTS:	YES: ☐ NO: ☐	STAFF NAME: SIGNED:

DATE	TIME	PERSON REFUSED	PRODUCT/COMMENTS	AGED FOR ID	REFUSED BY/SIGNED
....../....../......	:	MALE................ ☐ FEMALE.............. ☐	REASON: COMMENTS:	YES: ☐ NO: ☐	STAFF NAME: SIGNED:

DATE	TIME	PERSON REFUSED	PRODUCT/COMMENTS	AGED FOR ID	REFUSED BY/SIGNED
....../....../......	:	MALE................ ☐ FEMALE.............. ☐	REASON: COMMENTS:	YES: ☐ NO: ☐	STAFF NAME: SIGNED:

DATE	TIME	PERSON REFUSED	PRODUCT/COMMENTS	AGED FOR ID	REFUSED BY/SIGNED
....../....../......	:	MALE................ ☐ FEMALE.............. ☐	REASON: COMMENTS:	YES: ☐ NO: ☐	STAFF NAME: SIGNED:

CHALLENGE 25
Records of refusals

🚫18

DATE	TIME	PERSON REFUSED	PRODUCT/COMMENTS	AGED FOR ID	REFUSED BY/SIGNED
....../....../......	:	MALE..................☐ FEMALE..............☐	REASON: COMMENTS:	YES: ☐ NO: ☐	STAFF NAME: SIGNED:

DATE	TIME	PERSON REFUSED	PRODUCT/COMMENTS	AGED FOR ID	REFUSED BY/SIGNED
....../....../......	:	MALE..................☐ FEMALE..............☐	REASON: COMMENTS:	YES: ☐ NO: ☐	STAFF NAME: SIGNED:

DATE	TIME	PERSON REFUSED	PRODUCT/COMMENTS	AGED FOR ID	REFUSED BY/SIGNED
....../....../......	:	MALE..................☐ FEMALE..............☐	REASON: COMMENTS:	YES: ☐ NO: ☐	STAFF NAME: SIGNED:

DATE	TIME	PERSON REFUSED	PRODUCT/COMMENTS	AGED FOR ID	REFUSED BY/SIGNED
....../....../......	:	MALE..................☐ FEMALE..............☐	REASON: COMMENTS:	YES: ☐ NO: ☐	STAFF NAME: SIGNED:

DATE	TIME	PERSON REFUSED	PRODUCT/COMMENTS	AGED FOR ID	REFUSED BY/SIGNED
....../....../......	:	MALE..................☐ FEMALE..............☐	REASON: COMMENTS:	YES: ☐ NO: ☐	STAFF NAME: SIGNED:

DATE	TIME	PERSON REFUSED	PRODUCT/COMMENTS	AGED FOR ID	REFUSED BY/SIGNED
....../....../......	:	MALE..................☐ FEMALE..............☐	REASON: COMMENTS:	YES: ☐ NO: ☐	STAFF NAME: SIGNED:

CHALLENGE 25
Records of refusals

(18)

DATE	TIME	PERSON REFUSED	PRODUCT/COMMENTS	AGED FOR ID	REFUSED BY/SIGNED
....../ ....../	:	MALE................☐ FEMALE.............☐	REASON: COMMENTS:	YES: ☐ NO: ☐	STAFF NAME: SIGNED:

DATE	TIME	PERSON REFUSED	PRODUCT/COMMENTS	AGED FOR ID	REFUSED BY/SIGNED
....../ ....../	:	MALE................☐ FEMALE.............☐	REASON: COMMENTS:	YES: ☐ NO: ☐	STAFF NAME: SIGNED:

DATE	TIME	PERSON REFUSED	PRODUCT/COMMENTS	AGED FOR ID	REFUSED BY/SIGNED
....../ ....../	:	MALE................☐ FEMALE.............☐	REASON: COMMENTS:	YES: ☐ NO: ☐	STAFF NAME: SIGNED:

DATE	TIME	PERSON REFUSED	PRODUCT/COMMENTS	AGED FOR ID	REFUSED BY/SIGNED
....../ ....../	:	MALE................☐ FEMALE.............☐	REASON: COMMENTS:	YES: ☐ NO: ☐	STAFF NAME: SIGNED:

DATE	TIME	PERSON REFUSED	PRODUCT/COMMENTS	AGED FOR ID	REFUSED BY/SIGNED
....../ ....../	:	MALE................☐ FEMALE.............☐	REASON: COMMENTS:	YES: ☐ NO: ☐	STAFF NAME: SIGNED:

DATE	TIME	PERSON REFUSED	PRODUCT/COMMENTS	AGED FOR ID	REFUSED BY/SIGNED
....../ ....../	:	MALE................☐ FEMALE.............☐	REASON: COMMENTS:	YES: ☐ NO: ☐	STAFF NAME: SIGNED:

CHALLENGE 25
Records of refusals

DATE	TIME	PERSON REFUSED	PRODUCT/COMMENTS	AGED FOR ID	REFUSED BY/SIGNED
....../....../.......	:	MALE................ ☐ FEMALE............. ☐	REASON: COMMENTS:	YES: ☐ NO: ☐	STAFF NAME: SIGNED:

DATE	TIME	PERSON REFUSED	PRODUCT/COMMENTS	AGED FOR ID	REFUSED BY/SIGNED
....../....../.......	:	MALE................ ☐ FEMALE............. ☐	REASON: COMMENTS:	YES: ☐ NO: ☐	STAFF NAME: SIGNED:

DATE	TIME	PERSON REFUSED	PRODUCT/COMMENTS	AGED FOR ID	REFUSED BY/SIGNED
....../....../.......	:	MALE................ ☐ FEMALE............. ☐	REASON: COMMENTS:	YES: ☐ NO: ☐	STAFF NAME: SIGNED:

DATE	TIME	PERSON REFUSED	PRODUCT/COMMENTS	AGED FOR ID	REFUSED BY/SIGNED
....../....../.......	:	MALE................ ☐ FEMALE............. ☐	REASON: COMMENTS:	YES: ☐ NO: ☐	STAFF NAME: SIGNED:

DATE	TIME	PERSON REFUSED	PRODUCT/COMMENTS	AGED FOR ID	REFUSED BY/SIGNED
....../....../.......	:	MALE................ ☐ FEMALE............. ☐	REASON: COMMENTS:	YES: ☐ NO: ☐	STAFF NAME: SIGNED:

DATE	TIME	PERSON REFUSED	PRODUCT/COMMENTS	AGED FOR ID	REFUSED BY/SIGNED
....../....../.......	:	MALE................ ☐ FEMALE............. ☐	REASON: COMMENTS:	YES: ☐ NO: ☐	STAFF NAME: SIGNED:

CHALLENGE 25
Records of refusals

DATE	TIME	PERSON REFUSED	PRODUCT/COMMENTS	AGED FOR ID	REFUSED BY/SIGNED
....../....../......	:	MALE................ ☐ FEMALE.............. ☐	REASON: COMMENTS:	YES: ☐ NO: ☐	STAFF NAME: SIGNED:

DATE	TIME	PERSON REFUSED	PRODUCT/COMMENTS	AGED FOR ID	REFUSED BY/SIGNED
....../....../......	:	MALE................ ☐ FEMALE.............. ☐	REASON: COMMENTS:	YES: ☐ NO: ☐	STAFF NAME: SIGNED:

DATE	TIME	PERSON REFUSED	PRODUCT/COMMENTS	AGED FOR ID	REFUSED BY/SIGNED
....../....../......	:	MALE................ ☐ FEMALE.............. ☐	REASON: COMMENTS:	YES: ☐ NO: ☐	STAFF NAME: SIGNED:

DATE	TIME	PERSON REFUSED	PRODUCT/COMMENTS	AGED FOR ID	REFUSED BY/SIGNED
....../....../......	:	MALE................ ☐ FEMALE.............. ☐	REASON: COMMENTS:	YES: ☐ NO: ☐	STAFF NAME: SIGNED:

DATE	TIME	PERSON REFUSED	PRODUCT/COMMENTS	AGED FOR ID	REFUSED BY/SIGNED
....../....../......	:	MALE................ ☐ FEMALE.............. ☐	REASON: COMMENTS:	YES: ☐ NO: ☐	STAFF NAME: SIGNED:

DATE	TIME	PERSON REFUSED	PRODUCT/COMMENTS	AGED FOR ID	REFUSED BY/SIGNED
....../....../......	:	MALE................ ☐ FEMALE.............. ☐	REASON: COMMENTS:	YES: ☐ NO: ☐	STAFF NAME: SIGNED:

CHALLENGE 25
Records of refusals

DATE	TIME	PERSON REFUSED	PRODUCT/COMMENTS	AGED FOR ID	REFUSED BY/SIGNED
....../....../.......	:	MALE...................☐ FEMALE...............☐	REASON: COMMENTS:	YES: ☐ NO: ☐	STAFF NAME: SIGNED:

DATE	TIME	PERSON REFUSED	PRODUCT/COMMENTS	AGED FOR ID	REFUSED BY/SIGNED
....../....../.......	:	MALE...................☐ FEMALE...............☐	REASON: COMMENTS:	YES: ☐ NO: ☐	STAFF NAME: SIGNED:

DATE	TIME	PERSON REFUSED	PRODUCT/COMMENTS	AGED FOR ID	REFUSED BY/SIGNED
....../....../.......	:	MALE...................☐ FEMALE...............☐	REASON: COMMENTS:	YES: ☐ NO: ☐	STAFF NAME: SIGNED:

DATE	TIME	PERSON REFUSED	PRODUCT/COMMENTS	AGED FOR ID	REFUSED BY/SIGNED
....../....../.......	:	MALE...................☐ FEMALE...............☐	REASON: COMMENTS:	YES: ☐ NO: ☐	STAFF NAME: SIGNED:

DATE	TIME	PERSON REFUSED	PRODUCT/COMMENTS	AGED FOR ID	REFUSED BY/SIGNED
....../....../.......	:	MALE...................☐ FEMALE...............☐	REASON: COMMENTS:	YES: ☐ NO: ☐	STAFF NAME: SIGNED:

DATE	TIME	PERSON REFUSED	PRODUCT/COMMENTS	AGED FOR ID	REFUSED BY/SIGNED
....../....../.......	:	MALE...................☐ FEMALE...............☐	REASON: COMMENTS:	YES: ☐ NO: ☐	STAFF NAME: SIGNED:

CHALLENGE 25
Records of refusals

DATE	TIME	PERSON REFUSED	PRODUCT/COMMENTS	AGED FOR ID	REFUSED BY/SIGNED
......./......./.......	:	MALE................... ☐ FEMALE............... ☐	REASON: COMMENTS:	YES: ☐ NO: ☐	STAFF NAME: SIGNED:

DATE	TIME	PERSON REFUSED	PRODUCT/COMMENTS	AGED FOR ID	REFUSED BY/SIGNED
......./......./.......	:	MALE................... ☐ FEMALE............... ☐	REASON: COMMENTS:	YES: ☐ NO: ☐	STAFF NAME: SIGNED:

DATE	TIME	PERSON REFUSED	PRODUCT/COMMENTS	AGED FOR ID	REFUSED BY/SIGNED
......./......./.......	:	MALE................... ☐ FEMALE............... ☐	REASON: COMMENTS:	YES: ☐ NO: ☐	STAFF NAME: SIGNED:

DATE	TIME	PERSON REFUSED	PRODUCT/COMMENTS	AGED FOR ID	REFUSED BY/SIGNED
......./......./.......	:	MALE................... ☐ FEMALE............... ☐	REASON: COMMENTS:	YES: ☐ NO: ☐	STAFF NAME: SIGNED:

DATE	TIME	PERSON REFUSED	PRODUCT/COMMENTS	AGED FOR ID	REFUSED BY/SIGNED
......./......./.......	:	MALE................... ☐ FEMALE............... ☐	REASON: COMMENTS:	YES: ☐ NO: ☐	STAFF NAME: SIGNED:

DATE	TIME	PERSON REFUSED	PRODUCT/COMMENTS	AGED FOR ID	REFUSED BY/SIGNED
......./......./.......	:	MALE................... ☐ FEMALE............... ☐	REASON: COMMENTS:	YES: ☐ NO: ☐	STAFF NAME: SIGNED:

CHALLENGE 25
Records of refusals

DATE	TIME	PERSON REFUSED	PRODUCT/COMMENTS	AGED FOR ID	REFUSED BY/SIGNED
....../....../......	:	MALE.................. ☐ FEMALE..............☐	REASON: COMMENTS:	YES: ☐ NO: ☐	STAFF NAME: SIGNED:

DATE	TIME	PERSON REFUSED	PRODUCT/COMMENTS	AGED FOR ID	REFUSED BY/SIGNED
....../....../......	:	MALE.................. ☐ FEMALE..............☐	REASON: COMMENTS:	YES: ☐ NO: ☐	STAFF NAME: SIGNED:

DATE	TIME	PERSON REFUSED	PRODUCT/COMMENTS	AGED FOR ID	REFUSED BY/SIGNED
....../....../......	:	MALE.................. ☐ FEMALE..............☐	REASON: COMMENTS:	YES: ☐ NO: ☐	STAFF NAME: SIGNED:

DATE	TIME	PERSON REFUSED	PRODUCT/COMMENTS	AGED FOR ID	REFUSED BY/SIGNED
....../....../......	:	MALE.................. ☐ FEMALE..............☐	REASON: COMMENTS:	YES: ☐ NO: ☐	STAFF NAME: SIGNED:

DATE	TIME	PERSON REFUSED	PRODUCT/COMMENTS	AGED FOR ID	REFUSED BY/SIGNED
....../....../......	:	MALE.................. ☐ FEMALE..............☐	REASON: COMMENTS:	YES: ☐ NO: ☐	STAFF NAME: SIGNED:

DATE	TIME	PERSON REFUSED	PRODUCT/COMMENTS	AGED FOR ID	REFUSED BY/SIGNED
....../....../......	:	MALE.................. ☐ FEMALE..............☐	REASON: COMMENTS:	YES: ☐ NO: ☐	STAFF NAME: SIGNED:

CHALLENGE 25
Records of refusals

DATE	TIME	PERSON REFUSED	PRODUCT/COMMENTS	AGED FOR ID	REFUSED BY/SIGNED
....../ ....../	:	MALE.................. ☐ FEMALE.............. ☐	REASON: COMMENTS:	YES: ☐ NO: ☐	STAFF NAME: SIGNED:

DATE	TIME	PERSON REFUSED	PRODUCT/COMMENTS	AGED FOR ID	REFUSED BY/SIGNED
....../ ....../	:	MALE.................. ☐ FEMALE.............. ☐	REASON: COMMENTS:	YES: ☐ NO: ☐	STAFF NAME: SIGNED:

DATE	TIME	PERSON REFUSED	PRODUCT/COMMENTS	AGED FOR ID	REFUSED BY/SIGNED
....../ ....../	:	MALE.................. ☐ FEMALE.............. ☐	REASON: COMMENTS:	YES: ☐ NO: ☐	STAFF NAME: SIGNED:

DATE	TIME	PERSON REFUSED	PRODUCT/COMMENTS	AGED FOR ID	REFUSED BY/SIGNED
....../ ....../	:	MALE.................. ☐ FEMALE.............. ☐	REASON: COMMENTS:	YES: ☐ NO: ☐	STAFF NAME: SIGNED:

DATE	TIME	PERSON REFUSED	PRODUCT/COMMENTS	AGED FOR ID	REFUSED BY/SIGNED
....../ ....../	:	MALE.................. ☐ FEMALE.............. ☐	REASON: COMMENTS:	YES: ☐ NO: ☐	STAFF NAME: SIGNED:

DATE	TIME	PERSON REFUSED	PRODUCT/COMMENTS	AGED FOR ID	REFUSED BY/SIGNED
....../ ....../	:	MALE.................. ☐ FEMALE.............. ☐	REASON: COMMENTS:	YES: ☐ NO: ☐	STAFF NAME: SIGNED:

Printed in Great Britain
by Amazon